The Clinical Case in Psychoanalysis

The Clinical Case in Psychoanalysis explores the question of what makes a "case" in psychoanalysis, more than a century after Freud invented analytic treatment.

Luis Izcovich brings a Lacanian perspective to this important issue, asking under what conditions we can affirm that a case is a case of the psychoanalytic clinic. Izcovich examines the evolution of clinical vignettes in contemporary psychoanalysis, critically assessing how analysts present their own clinical experiences. Through rigorous analysis, he questions established psychoanalytic practices, demonstrating the profound clinical effects of analytic interpretation and the transformative impact of the psychoanalytic experience. Drawing extensively on Lacan's teachings, this book reveals why understanding clinical structure as just one dimension of a case represents a crucial advancement in psychoanalytic thought.

The Clinical Case in Psychoanalysis will be essential reading for clinicians and scholars seeking to deepen their understanding of psychoanalytic case formulation and therapeutic efficacy.

Luis Izcovich is a psychiatrist and psychoanalyst based in Paris. He is a founding member of the EPFCL (École de Psychanalyse des Forums du Champ Lacanien). He also serves as the Director of Editions Stilus and teaches psychoanalysis at the Clinical College of Psychoanalysis in Paris. His extensive scholarly work includes numerous books published in multiple languages including English, French, Spanish, Italian, and Portuguese.

The Clinical Case in Psychoanalysis

A Lacanian Perspective

Luis Izcovich

Translated by
Patrick Boulard

Routledge
Taylor & Francis Group

LONDON AND NEW YORK

Designed cover image: Getty | Dmytro Synelnychenko

First published 2026
by Routledge
4 Park Square, Milton Park, Abingdon, Oxon OX14 4RN

and by Routledge
605 Third Avenue, New York, NY 10158

Routledge is an imprint of the Taylor & Francis Group, an informa business

© 2026 Luis Izcovich

British Library Cataloguing in Publication Data
A catalogue record for this book is available from the British Library

ISBN: 978-1-032-93935-3 (hbk)
ISBN: 978-1-032-90192-3 (pbk)
ISBN: 978-1-003-56831-5 (ebk)

DOI: 10.4324/9781003568315

Typeset in Times New Roman
by Taylor & Francis Books

Contents

Introduction

More than a century after Freud invented the mechanism of the analytical treatment, there still is *a* question: what is exactly a case in psychoanalysis?

This question arises all the more so, since Lacan himself never made use of this appellation of *case* to refer to a hospital presentation of patients, and nowadays the most frequent use to communicate the analytical clinic is that of *clinical vignette*. Besides, and widely spread almost everywhere, when someone pretends to transmit the analysis experience, there exists for analysts a practice aiming to present several cases issued from their own clinical experience, in order to comment on how phenomena appear in analytical clinic and subsequently what the analyst may answer.

From this a relevant fundamental question arises: how can we assert that a case is a case based on psychoanalytic clinic?

As we know, the presentation of patients and cases finds its source in medicine, and Freud – as well as Lacan – was involved in this history.

It becomes essential to know how for psychoanalysis they made use of it, and since then, to focus on what has changed in order to draw out the consequences for the analytical clinic and its transmission today.

Initially, Freud chose narration as a method of transmission of the clinic. A few years and a day-to-day development of the analytical mechanism were necessary to move from short case narrative – as attested by his first hysterical patients – towards what he calls with Dora's case, a "snippet of a clinical history".[1] It is the beginning of a process meant to deliver a history turning over his patient's symptoms. The aim had always intended to demonstrate the sexual trauma coming about during infancy, and how this trauma exercised its effect through symptoms, and the efficiency of analytical interpretation under transference. He carried on this method but not exclusively, out of his analytical practice. Thus, he mentions writers, historical annals of the religion, like "Une névrose démoniaque au XVIIe siècle" [A 17th Century Demonic Neurosis], or a lawyer's memoirs as in the "Schreber case". Nevertheless, the essentials of his transmission came through his own practice, and his choice of German Romanticism as a layout was sustained by the context of his times.

DOI: 10.4324/9781003568315-1

Thus, gradually one may assist to Freud's attempt to transmit the most thorough clinic, without loss, even incorporating his own notes as in "The Rat Man, Some Remarks on a Case of Obsessive-Compulsive Neurosis", and drafting at night after each session out of what he had retained from his patient. We perceive Freud's dual choices, one being inspired by the literature of his time, the other resulting from his scientific training.

Undoubtedly, Freud made use of a narrative mode for the transmission of a case. Several so-called post-Freudian analysts followed the same path, but Lacan never did. Others abandoned narration for description. Just observe how Melanie Klein and her students were emphatic on the details about someone's appearance, corporeality, and apparel. However, to be able to prove the existence of the unconscious and its potential effects through verbal communication in analysis, Freud often addressed to an Other among the scientific community.

With Lacan, you notice the same worry, but this time addressed to somebody else. The epoch had changed and it was no longer necessary to obtain an acknowledgement from science. The Unconscious had already gained the right to exist. Nevertheless, Lacan never ceased to demonstrate what may be called an analytical effect. To be true, if Lacan switches interlocutors, he does not modify his goal: the transmission of what is exactly an analysis, in order to diffuse the analytic discourse. His appeal to the clinical transmission is no longer the grand *Historial*, that it had been previously for Freud. It is the reason why, most often, Lacan is opposed to Freud because of his choice to operate an extreme reduction of transmission. This opposition seems legitimate.

It's a fact that Lacan introduced strict limits in his commentaries of cases, to the point that they could be explained in a single sentence. One has to relate to two cases only by the end of their analysis, as discussed in "Proposition of 9 October 1967 on the Psychoanalyst of the School". Each one is synthesized as a means to focus onto what became the subject's relationship to "object *a*", cause of desire: the voice for one, the gaze for the other.

Regarding the first case, Lacan formulated it like that: "Thus from him who received the key to the world in the split of the pre-pubescent, the psychoanalyst has no longer to expect a look, but sees himself become a voice".[2] And, for the second one, he poses:

> And this other who as a child found ideational representative in its irruption across the unfolded newspaper behind which the sewage farm of his progenitor's thoughts shelter, refers the effect of anxiety where he seesaws in his own dejection to the psychoanalyst.[3]

It is precisely at that time that Lacan's choice of the method to figure out the case by the end of an analysis involves the analyst's outcome. This is an unprecedented move for the analytical clinic.

Since Freud, the analyst has often been involved in the case narrative, but differently. Hence in Dora's case, Freud afterwards realized that the treatment turned up a dead-end, because of his own biases. Rapidly, out of his own experience, Freud understood that the analyst's feelings, ideas, and even knowledge, can hamper a treatment. Since Freud, some analytic movements have implicated the analyst in the record of a case, from the theorization of counter-transference.

Sometimes even the narrative of an ending treatment included the analyst's involvements. If Lacan's case narrative insofar is unprecedented, it's because the analyst is involved in the analysand's perspective. In other words, what's essential is the way the case is formulated and how it articulates itself out of the connection between the analysand's traumatic scenes, and for the analysand what becomes of the analyst at the end of the treatment. Among others, it's the aim we intend to demonstrate in this book.

It is noteworthy that when we emphasize the contrast between Freud and Lacan, we operate an all too massive opposition. Actually, after his 1918 French publication of the Wolf Man's case, and until the end, Freud never again published a single case aimed at reporting the wholeness of a story. After that date, Freud's references to the clinic are not missing, yet his style is different. Henceforth, he made use of short examples to demonstrate a point of theory, even if it was to distinguish between two clinical forms. That's how, for the young homosexual, he does not disclose any details about her infantile history. It's also patent in his text "Some Neurotic Mechanisms in Jealousy, Homosexuality, and Paranoia", where Freud in a very condensed form, relies on the subject's relationship to the father to distinguish neurosis and psychosis. In other words, Freud abandons the method aiming to express the most accurate narrative. It is not fortuitous that Freud's modality of transmission changed from the years coinciding in 1920 with the decline of analytical interpretation. The golden age of the discovery of the unconscious was behind him. Freud realized that psychoanalysis could move on, so long as it focused on what was said about analysis. It's probably the beginning for analysis of what Lacan posed as, *"the ethic of the well-spoken"*. Thus, he answered to a question posed to the analyst: *"what must I do?"*: *"for me [...] the reply is simple. Deriving from my practice the ethic of the well-spoken"*.[4] This was to demonstrate that the essential is not what's being said, but in the discourse how the *"spoken words"* [*les dits*] are structured, then he adds: *"an ethic is relative to a discourse"*.[5] Thereby, while for his cases Freud had or had not looked for personal details of infantile neurosis, he abandons this approach for the young homosexual. He essentially made use of this case to demonstrate that the unconscious is able to lie. Obviously out of this case, multiple other teachings are to be drawn out. Among them Lacan finds the passage to the act [*passage à l'acte*] conjuncture. Nevertheless, we can notice the *exit* of the grand narration.

Therefore it should be noted that, between 1918 and 1938, Freud is not the same clinician he had been before and it's a fact that his analysis lengthened in time. Another shift can be perceived. Freud no longer reported his involvements, nor the subject's improvements towards transference. It's true that Lacan, unlike Freud at his beginnings, does not have recourse to clinical narrations, but we cannot assert that Lacan's method is very divergent from Freud's method over its last 20 years.

Lacan's example, to illustrate the end of an analysis for an obsessive subject, demonstrates it, and this from the effects of a dream onto this analysand, as related by his female partner.[6]

This case narrative organizes itself, according to the method Freud is making use of during the second part of his practice. Actually, it informs about the clinic of obsessive neurosis, but it fails to figure out the case singularity. To be exact, that is for Lacan the ultimate reference authorizing him to situate the details of a case in his practice. Here and again, it is a demonstration of the way Lacan focuses the clinic of this period over the clinical structure. Yet, it is something else to talk about the case-based clinic as a clinic of singularity. That's the second goal we'll demonstrate throughout this book.

You must above all realize that Lacan's method remains essentially Freudian, in the sense that his reference to the clinic aims to demonstrate the manifestations of the unconscious, their link to language, the way they pass across the subject, and the combinations the unconscious creates in terms of desire.

On the other hand, Lacan does not abandon the Freudian's narrations. Instead, he aims to extract out of one case how to demonstrate a set. First, he attempts to figure out the case specificity, then to demonstrate its structure. Thus, he makes use of a case to extract what sets it apart, and at the same time what it shares with similar ones.

That's the axis of our teaching practices, the relationship between the case and the structure of the clinic. Generally, if we take the whole of Lacan's teaching since Freud, a historical step has taken place. We've moved in the clinic from an inquiry based on the case history, to what constitutes its substance. Thus, we switch from particularity to singularity. Does it mean that Freud exposed the particularity of an analysis and Lacan its singularity? I propose to demonstrate that this would constitute an unfair opposition.

It's true to say that Lacan went beyond the practice of commenting on cases, which for Freud had been a reference. He tried to isolate what could for each case be elevated to the category of paradigm. We may in this series insert his commentaries about cases related through post-Freudian movements. Each time, Lacan tried to highlight what a case demonstrates as a progress for the psychoanalysis practice, but also as hindrances and dead-ends, so one may make use of a case to enlighten oneself about other cases.

It must be mentioned that the practice which defines the essence of a case with a minimum of signifiers comes from Freud, in his attempt to name the subject's symptom in its most original version. Maybe it's with The Rat Man that Freud got the closest. He clears what makes the symptom in the case structure, what constitutes his fundamental symptom, and what was the leading fantasy of the subject's existence, but more fundamentally, Freud clears the name of the symptom, the signifier which gives the subject's identity, thereby establishing a relation of exception to the *jouissance*. It's what justifies its title to The Rat Man. One which makes exception. From this case, Freud moved from particular to singular. He not only names a case to recognize it. Here, the name is of service to figure out the horror of an enigmatic *jouissance* lurking in the subject's economy, and constitutes the case specificity.

Yet, Lacan went further and didn't stick to demonstrating how a case shares common features with other ones. It meant handling the clinical structure.

It's one of the reasons which justifies this book. It would be a deviation from the psychoanalytical option if, when one refers to a case in psychoanalysis, one restricts to a diagnostic of structure. Nevertheless, to figure out the clinical structure, one sometimes restricts the scope of the preliminary interviews, and even the debates about cases by the end of analysis.

It is rather about following Lacan's course of action. He always tried to prove what he retained as convincing about the analytical clinic, namely how a signifying articulation reduced to its minimal utterance can nevertheless say something about desire. Hence, Lacan's reference to the term of *paradigm*.

Thus, in the last part of his teaching, surprisingly, he goes back to Freud the analyst, in *The Interpretation of Dreams*, and makes use of the Witty Butcher's Wife's case, to call it a paradigmatic one.

Actually, in "The Direction of the Treatment and the Principles of its Power", Lacan proposes to slide this case under "the microscope" in order to highlight the subject's genuine and unconscious desire. It brings out an unnoticed and unknown dimension, going a step further than Freud's case interpretation. Precisely what Lacan demonstrates, is how Freud with his case interpretation resolved the pre-conscious desire. Lacan adds the unconscious dimension of desire linked to the subject's identification to the phallus. A microscopic detail sheds light on the case. It's striking. This is a case stemming from Freud's outset upon which he does not forge even a fragmentary history. He gives no detail of the infantile neurosis, even biographical. There is no feature telling what happened in the former generation. In other words, Freud neglects to transmit an anamnesis.

There is only a dream, its associations, the immediate context preceding the dream, and a few components linking the patient to his husband, and to a very close friend. But it was enough for Lacan to consider this case as paradigmatic. There lies a question about the method of transmission. It highlights desire in hysteria, as beyond its demand, linked to the phallus, whose end is to remain unsatisfied. It is the paradigm of desire in a clinical structure.

The case-based clinic pertains to another level. The case does not establish the universal, but much more how the exception enables to seize what makes the essence of the analytical clinic. The case therefore is not deprived of the structure, but goes beyond it. That beyond of the structure reveals, when it's possible, on the one hand the distance between the approach of a clinical case based on the scientific perspective to which belong psychology and psychiatry, and on the other the approach of the Lacanian guideline of psychoanalysis. That is our aim in this book.

Notes

1 Freud, S., "Fragment d'une analyse d'hystérie (Dora)", Cinq psychanalyses, Paris, PUF, 2006.
2 Lacan, J., "Proposition du 9 Octobre 1967 sur le psychanalyste de l'Ecole", in Autres écrits, Paris, Le Seuil, 2001, p. 254. ("Proposition of 9 October 1967 on the Psychoanalyst of the School". Translation by R. Grigg, pp. 10–13.)
3 Lacan, J., "Proposition du 9 Octobre 1967 sur le psychanalyste de l'Ecole", in Autres écrits, Paris, Le Seuil, 2001, p. 255. ("Proposition of 9 October 1967 on the Psychoanalyst of the School". Translation by R. Grigg, pp. 10–13.)
4 Lacan, J., "Télévision", in Autres écrits, Paris, Le Seuil, p. 541. (Television: A Challenge to the Psychoanalysis Establishment. Translation by J. Mehlman, New York and London, W.W. Norton, 1990, pp. 47–154.)
5 Lacan, J., "Télévision", in Autres écrits, Paris, Le Seuil, p. 541. (Television: A Challenge to the Psychoanalysis Establishment. Translation by J. Mehlman, New York and London, W.W. Norton, 1990. pp. 65–154.)
6 Lacan, J., "La direction de la cure et les principes de son pouvoir", in Écrits, Paris, Le Seuil, 1966, pp. 632–633. (The Direction of the Treatment and the Principles of its Power. Translation by B. Fink in collaboration with H. Fink and R. Grigg, New York and London, W.W. Norton and Company, 2002, pp. 630–631.)

Chapter 1

A Clinic Like No Others

A Chatter Practice

Psychoanalysis takes root in the emergence of a scientific discourse. Freud often chose a scientist as interlocutor, however he never concluded that psychoanalysis was a science. Lacan, who tried to display how science banishes any subjective dimension, concludes that there exists an analytical clinic, but it is a practice. He nevertheless kept up with the scientific advancements of his time, even asking himself what a science including psychoanalysis would look like. To pose it as a non-science introduces immediately the idea that the analytical clinic differs in its approach from the medical and psychiatric clinics, even if it is based upon both of them.

Even more, the scientific perspective makes use of academic discourse, and therefore relies on the most exact transmission with the minimal possible loss. It is the model followed by Freud in The Wolfman, when he tried to figure out the date of the traumatic scene, regarding the intercourse intervened between his parents that Serguëi Pankejeff – Freud's patient – would have attended.

If psychoanalysis is not a science, however, it would be appropriate to seize the driving pattern out of which it finds its way to transmit its discourse. In this book, my purpose will be to demonstrate that this pattern is the paradigm.

Indeed, in Lacan's outlined program for psychoanalysis, the paradigm takes place simultaneously to figure out what a case addresses about its clinic efficacy, and its value as transmission. This program is deducible as soon as Lacan poses singularity as an axis for psychoanalysis. Actually, in psychoanalysis we pose the case as *the* beyond of the clinical structure. The case is the transition from particular to singular.

Psychoanalysis stands on the fact that the clinic operates on the edge of a bed, wherefrom emerges the analytical clinic which operates on a couch. But the main thing is not there. Nowadays, the fact is that many analytical sessions take place face-to-face, for lying on a couch is not a guarantee for an analytical process. In his last seminar "Time to Conclude", once again Lacan

DOI: 10.4324/9781003568315-2

considers psychoanalysis as a non-science. This time, what's interesting is how Lacan justifies the pertinence of psychoanalysis, since he adds that it is "a chatter practice"[1] using the etymology of *bavardage* [chatter] and a witticism [the verb "*baver*"], he even adds "*postillonner*" [splutter].

It properly demonstrates how the speaker – the analysand – must be led to address his demand. In other words, the analysis does not mean a banal speech uttered by anyone. "Chatter" implies the whole phonatory apparatus, and therefore the body. It was not the first usage of this word. It was not innocent either, that Lacan long before had made use of it when he introduced an ethics specific to psychoanalysis.

Hence, he argued: "An ethics arises, converted to silence, not by way of fear, but of desire; and the question is how analysis' pathway of chatter leads to it".[2]

Therefore, being a practice of speech does not mean blabbering. It is why immediately after having stated that "chatter" is a practice, Lacan formulated: "it must lead to consequences"[3] [*elle doit porter à conséquence*].

Indeed, "chatter" is the only approach to seize the inadequacy between words and things, between what one wants to say, the intention, and what one is really saying. It is the attempt to bring the word up to the status of the thing, and as such, chatter constitutes a demanding practice wherein the analyst argues with his analysand about the importance to speak with his gut, and to be able to grab whatever stands at the very boundary between what's possible and impossible to say.

Therefore, Lacan poses chatter in its link to desire, to the speech and its effectiveness for anyone who commits oneself in this experience of speaking, and involves oneself in one's "spoken-words" [*dits*]. Even more, as said before, chatter articulates itself onto the analyst's silence, and is led by what founds the analytic ethics, namely that speaking may have an effect on desire. It is only on this path that there is a chance to seize what a case-based clinic is.

I resume: psychoanalysis is a case-based clinic in that it strives for the singular. Clinic of the particular and clinic of the singular must be differentiated. In a set, the particular is the common element. When by the end of his teachings, Lacan reverts to the symptom, he poses: "there is consistency between the symptom and the unconscious. Except for the fact that the symptom cannot be defined otherwise than by the way in which each one enjoys the unconscious in so far as the unconscious determines it".[4]

The everyone is meant as a reference which perforce involves *the* wholeness. Everyone has a symptom and it makes everyone suffer his own way. That leads to something no less momentous:

> in every case, of his unconscious and the way in which he enjoys it, the symptom remains at the same place that Marx put it, but it takes on a different meaning. It is not a social symptom, it is a particular symptom.

No doubt, these particular symptoms have types, and the symptom of the obsessional is not the symptom of the hysteric.[5]

Here, it is explicit, the symptom is particular in the sense that it connects to a clinical structure. Singularity is something else. It is determined by the marks of infantile *jouissance*; they are always off-standard. And the analysis is precisely what sets up an expertise with this exception. In this sense, in a psychoanalysis, one switches from hidden singularity because of the subject's identifications, to an unveiled singularity. Here, one is at the level of the paradigmatic singularity and in psychoanalysis it is exactly what is involved in the case-based clinic.

In Lacan's teaching, from very early on, singularity is active through another bias. Already in *The Ethics of Psychoanalysis* and "The Direction of the Treatment and the Principles of its Power", Lacan refers to a singular judgement coming out of the analysand, but also necessary to the analyst's position. This judgement cannot proceed from a norm, but concerns somebody's intimate choice.

A year after *The Ethics of Psychoanalysis*, Lacan emphasizes it in "The Identification", when he formulates that what's at stake is not so much virtues of the norm than virtues of its exception.[6]

A norm is deduced from a universal rule and the exception does not prove it, but rather it is what makes objection. Therefrom, Lacan objects to Kant's idea of unity and introduces the notion of *The* One [*L'Un*], *The* One [*L'Un*] who incarnates oneself, playing with the French homophony of these two words "*Un*" and "*Incarne*". It is interesting to notice the latter etymology. *Incarnate* [*Incarner*] means to enter into the body, the flesh. Italian or Spanish is clearer, for flesh is *carne*. In other words, to obtain *The* One of singularity, there must be some signifier which penetrates into the body.

Actually, Lacan takes the step with his "Logic of fantasy", when he poses the Other, not as the Holy Spirit but as a signifier which incarnates into the body.

It demonstrates the existence of a necessity which is to appropriate some signifier, to make the signifier take shape. With *The* incarnating One [*L'Un*], we stand at the level of singularity. At the same time in "The Identification", Lacan, about desire, introduces the notion of a necessary difference, becoming later in *The Four Fundamental Concepts of Psychoanalysis*, the analyst's proper desire, that is to obtain the absolute difference. One notices that what is considered as capital is to seize singularity, the relationship between desire and body. Indeed, the desire requires that a signifier incarnates into the body.

The interest of referring to *The* One which incarnates, enables us to indicate that a gap between two signifiers is insufficient to enliven a desire, but that desire still needs what operates as a remainder, as a cause. On this point *The Four Fundamental Concepts of Psychoanalysis* provides the articulation between the original desire, and the absolute difference. Difference is indeed absolute if there has been a production of singularity. Therefrom, Lacan's conclusive remark in this seminar, which poses as a program to evaluate an analysis, is the way a subject lives the drive once they have traversed the fundamental fantasy.

Fantasy is everyone's and is an answer to the Other's desire. In that sense fantasy falls under the particular. It operates as a substrate to the subject. It is the particular of a desire vis-a-vis the universal.

What's striking in "The Identification", is Lacan referring to the particular and the universal in Kant; but he also seizes another dimension. Actually, beyond particular and universal judgements, Kant poses the existence of a singular one. According to his terms, Lacan demonstrates that Kant had left the singular judgement operating as a toothing-stone. One may notice, that the distinction between the particular and the singular was already existing.

The question is about the use of particular and singular in the experience of an analysis, and how the analysts translate it in the implementation of the proceedings of transmission. We may notice that in the cases' commentaries which are implemented in teaching structures, the particular concerns the clinic of subject. It aims to seize the signifiers a subject makes use of to be represented, and hence to situate himself in his existence. It is true that to be able to grab these signifiers, we have to understand how a subject organizes them within his own history. It raises a risk while conveying the transmission of a case, which is to stumble into a family romance. In psychoanalysis the case is not the subject's history being supplemented by some former generations' history. The romance founds itself in the myth. It's something else to bring out what a subject is possessing as most real. We'll come to it.

Before seizing the exception, let's discuss what would be the analytical norm. This one is noticeable in some post-Freudian options. For example, by establishing technical rules. Indeed, after Freud, the analysts tried to define some constants enabling them to fix the course of an analytical treatment. Hence, to be able to fix the conditions in which an analysis must be conducted, they have introduced several terms: setting, situation, pact, or analytical framework. Then, that notion widened to other technical requirements leading to the creation of analytical standards. A normative practice was born, deducible from Freud, but without any recommendation on his part.

But norm is not exclusively about technique. More fundamentally, the risk with norm is to standardize what can be expected from an analysis.

It is appropriate to follow the debate regarding an option of the analysis based on a norm, whose regulation and protocol would be elaborated by the Other, and Lacan's option which demonstrates the virtues of exception, the only guarantee to the analyst's act, and therefore to figure out what makes an identity for each one.

Therefore, our purpose will be to seize what is meant by a case-based clinic, which aims to figure out what makes exception and more fundamentally, how it differs from the narrative of a clinical history.

In psychoanalysis, a clinical case must be able to demonstrate the virtues of exception. Not only how the symptom is dissident regarding the norm, but also how the analyst's act is dissident regarding a knowledge filed in ortho- doxy. In this sense, we understand that psychoanalysis is a practice to reinvent endlessly, but which requires that we may demonstrate how a practice, which includes the unconscious, conveys some effects onto the desire. It is what we call an analytical effect.

Let's take Lacan's proposition about Little Hans' case. In *From an Other to the other*, Lacan underlines the fact that Little Hans would have sponta- neously healed of his phobia, without Freud's or his father's interventions and during the same period of time.

Precisely there, Lacan mentions "it goes well beyond the case"[7] to under- line that a case has to be seized beyond its signifying logic. For psycho- analysis, it is a real issue. Can one spontaneously heal one's symptom without an analysis? Sometimes analysands ask that question: "Is there any proof that healing is an effect of analysis and not only an effect of time?"

Undoubtedly, infantile neurosis as Little Hans' may spontaneously resolve itself, leaving a scar. Infantile neurosis solved without analysis should be set apart from neurosis which later on reactivates, and on the contrary always worsens over time. If Lacan evokes this, it is to make clear that the essential is not only that question of healing, but the relationship a subject is having "beyond the case", that is to say beyond the signifier, with "object *a*". So "beyond the case", means beyond the symbolic. The clinic of symbolic is that of subject. It finds its way from the position a subject is adopting within lan- guage, and of his relationship, to lack. The diagnostic tracking, limited to this perspective, often takes place with the handling of language: handling of language assorted to a certain elaboration suggests neurosis, while handling with a limited elaboration raises suspicion towards psychosis. We rapidly realize the limits of this approach. When Lacan asserts *the* "beyond the case", it clearly supposes that the connection to language is fundamental, but in this "beyond", what is worth is the subject's connection to lack of a signifier. How with regard to this lack does he take a stand? Therefrom springs up the importance given by Lacan to what is inside that the signifiers breach, the unspeakable, which appears as affects of real, particularly through anxiety. For it is by seizing the gap between the signifiers that there is a chance to bring out the desire.

For the subject, there is still the option to suffer from his symptoms, or otherwise to go through a demand for analysis.

In his "Introduction to a first volume of the *Écrits*", Lacan resumes the distinction between particular and singular, when he asserts:

By which I indicate that what arises from the same structure, does not necessarily have the same meaning. This is why there is only analysis of the particular: it is not at all that a same structure proceeds from a single meaning and above all not when the structure attains to discourse.[8]

This statement compels one to consider the three registers: real, symbolic, and imaginary, to resume the debate between universal and singular. Lacan operates an articulation which does not exclude either of them. The expression of *structure* which Lacan refers to, might be considered through two perspectives. Firstly, as being the structure of language. Indeed, all speaking beings are traversed by language (it's a universal), and yet the meaning is always specific to each one (it's the particular). However, Lacan adds up: "it is not at all that a same structure proceeds from a single meaning and above all not when the structure attains to discourse".[9]

One may consider the second perspective; the reference to the structure as a clinical structure. Since the particular indicates the subject within a set, here this set is the clinical structure.

When he formulates that "structure [...] attains to discourse", the implicit reference is the hysterical structure. That's indeed the only one which attains to the discourse insofar as Lacan posed the obsessional structure, and not the obsessional discourse. To reach the discourse, and step in analysis, the obsessive does it, but also through the hysterical discourse.

Let's come to the singular. It is the quantification of the unconscious *jouissance* which constitutes the singular, and stands it apart from the clinical structure which is a ranking mode of subjects in topics, with the illusion to share a common meaning.

Here should be recalled the nominalist point of view. It corresponds to that of the singularity, which goes against every kind of ranking system; for rankings are a signifying organization, which like any signifying organization is a system of semblances. That being said, structures exist. Structures are not semblance.

One should indeed consider the debate between nominalism and realism. Nominalism is case-by-case. It does not rule out the universal. Nominalism poses that there is nothing else than what a person perceives. One should refer to William of Ockham quoted by Pierre Alferi: "Singularity is the absolute as such, only heart of things, every being's (*étant*) coincidence with himself".[10] Thus, is delineated the essence of an objection to the universal.

I resume Lacan's text "Introduction to a first volume of the *Écrits*" where he poses the paradigm of desire:

> There is no common meaning of the hysteric, and the role played for them (eux ou elles) by identification is structure, and not meaning, as is clearly read in the fact that it bears on desire, on lack taken as an object, not on the cause of the lack. (Cf. the dream of the beautiful butcher's wife – in the Traumdeutung – become exemplary thanks to me. I am not

prodigal in my examples, but when I involve myself with them, I carry them to the paradigm.)[11]

Lacan is insistent to indicate, as in the former paragraph: "not the same meaning" or "not a unique meaning". Here, he reiterates again, stating: "no common meaning". It sends back to the understanding. Firstly, it tells us that what we know about a subject doesn't fit to another one, and secondly that a same phenomenon according to the subjects may have a different meaning. Finally, and objecting to the common meaning of hysteria, Lacan on this matter brings forward a decisive formulation.

He goes back to Freud's example, namely The Witty Butcher's Wife, and goes a step further. The Witty Butcher's Wife's dream is at length commented by Lacan in his "The Direction of the Treatment and the Principles of Its Power", from the subject's relationship to signifiers based on the need-demand-desire triad.

Lacan extracts out of Freud's case what is worth for the hysterical structure, and also for the structure of desire. Desire takes root in the Other's desire. In that sense, it is essential to keep to the fundamental part played in hysteria by identification. That is what Lacan brings forward until "Introduction...": the hysterical desires by proxy. That is also what founds the definition of hysteria as being a desire of an unsatisfied desire.

Yet, what is new here is the adjustment he operates to what's above, with his formulation "identification is structure, and not the fact that it bears on desire, on lack taken as an object, not on the cause of the lack".[12]

To identify with the cause of lack has already been posed by Freud with the hysterical identification. The case mentioned by Freud about a young girl in a convent, bursting into tears after having read the letter sent by her lover, and the similar effect produced on the other girls watching her, bears witness to this. It is as if each one had told herself, "If I had received such a letter, I would have responded the same way". The subject identifies to what is the cause of his misfortune. On the contrary, the formulation "on lack taken as an object" implies another level. It is not a transient identification as in the latter example, and neither an identification to the phallus, "even a somewhat skinny one", as Lacan makes it clear, taking one step further with regard to Freud.[13]

> "To identify to the lack taken as an object" indicates a modality of relationship to desire which in its essence implies that the object has to be missing. The hysteric worships the lack, it is her object. Lacan had already worded it as "The devotion of the hysteric, her passion for identifying with every sentimental drama".[14]

In this text I find that proposition consistent, which extends Lacan's new thesis about interpretation as it had been put forward the previous year, when he asserts that, in analysis, interpretation must be relevant to the cause of desire.[15]

This return to a case, out of Freud's early practice, doesn't imply the abandonment of the conception of the hysterical structure operating as desire of unsatisfied desire, but introduces another crucial level regarding what one may expect out of the analysis of hysteria, namely a renunciation to a sloppy love for lost causes.

Particular and singular

A case in psychoanalysis makes objection to any pre-established knowledge, and by a twofold manner. On the subject's side, its work in progress is unique. On the analyst's side, there is objection if the interpretation makes a hole [*fait trou*] in the subject's knowledge. It is defining an interpretation in analysis and inserts something new. Following that meaning, the case in psychoanalysis varies from its initial coordinates. It's verified when the new, an effect resulting from the interpretation, is by the end of the treatment brought up to produce the exception.

What Lacan brought forward about the unconscious and the symptom could be applied to a case. The analyst indeed is part of the concept of the unconscious, to the subject he is also a symptom partner and is embodied in the clinical case. Likewise, according to the unconscious and the symptom, the analyst completes the case. In other words, in analysis there is no case without the analyst's saying [*le dire de l'analyste*]. It highlights what makes a case in analysis, namely the exception, and the analyst is a part of it. It should be noticed that the exception remains an outlaw. In that sense, it is a real. Hence, the case-based clinic is a clinic of real, which is something else than developing elucubrations out of a case.

What it's about, is to grab on the subject's side what is non-compliant to the norm, plus in his acting the analyst's non-compliance. Still remains the question: who decides that what is said of a case is not a pure elucubration? There would be a response. It would be the consensus. But as this term suggests, one reaches consensus through a shared commitment. It is the principle of the meaning. It should be noticed that it is possible to obtain the other's commitment through suggestion. It is the reason why one moves away from elucubration as one seeks to demonstrate.

In other words, what is at odds with elucubration is the coherence. Nevertheless, if the coherence of transmission is what brings us closer to a clinic of real, to me it seems insufficient to sustain oneself in coherence. Coherence characterizes the academic discourse. This discourse, as we have said about scientific discourse with which it has affinities, is meant to aim at a transmission without loss.

Let's come to what seems to be the paradigm of a clinical transmission in psychoanalysis. It is about a case being transmitted through the procedure of the pass. In this clinic of the pass are considered the effects of analysis, up to their ultimate consequences onto desire. Let's develop this point.

From the signifying logic, Lacan ordains the treatment with two notions which possess commonalities, one is formatting the symptom, the other is the symptom's formal envelop. These two notions help to indicate the constitution and the future of analytical symptom.

In both cases, what matters is to ordain the clinic, according to the subject's position facing the insistence of repetition produced by infantile trauma. With both notions, Lacan tries to demonstrate how signifiers revolve around a nucleus. The signifying logic tries to capture the way a case organizes itself in regard of this center of gravity, to which Lacan at first gives the name of "object *a*", then of real.

To identify the signifying logic of course is of interest. But the signifying logic is not the whole logic of case. What the signifying logic does not capture, as we have said, is the gap between the particular and the singular. You grab the singular, if you grab what is heterogeneous to the signifying. What is heterogeneous is the subject's opaque *jouissance.*

It is moreover in this direction that Lacan introduced a modality of interpretation, which he qualified as intrusive. Indeed, it means that to define a case you must access inside the subject what operates radically as an insubordination to the Other, and how the analysis modifies the subject's relationship to this insubordination. The insubordination to the Other implies two dimensions. The first one is the signifying register. Indeed, it is from an assumed no to the Other, that one assumes one's own thought, but insubordination concerns a beyond. It falls under a *jouissance* which resists its symbolic grip.

In fact, one may argue that for psychoanalysis a case is a case, if one captures the subject's saying as an effect of the analyst's saying. Of course, the saying is captured by the end. Thence, the case template would be the saying that you extract out of the testimony of the pass. It is what Lacan highlights in the following phrasing:

> When one recognizes the sort of surplus enjoyment (*plus-de-jouir*) that makes one say "this (*ça*) is someone," one will be on the path of a dialectical material maybe more active than the flesh dedicated to a Party, being employed as the history's baby-sitter [in English]. This path, the psychoanalyst could light it with his pass.[16]

To be someone presumes a distinctive feature, a feature which constitutes a difference, therefore which is not common to everyone. That feature linked to *surplus-jouissance* [*plus-de-jouir*] indicates a specific modality of *jouissance*, spotted in the pass. For this one, this modality constitutes one's being [*l'être de ce quelqu'un*]. It is what's aimed at in the case-based clinic. That is something else than ideally to erase oneself for the best interest of the Party, which here is the Communist Party. Hence, the case would constitute one's being [*l'être de quelqu'un*]. If Lacan refers to the pass, it is because it eminently constitutes the mechanism enabling to highlight what a case is.

Clinic of real

In his interpretation of Freud's cases, Lacan handles them as a value of transmission of the clinic. A method holds a prominent position in the analysts' training; the reference to clinical cases. Hence, one tries to display pertinence of concepts or efficacy of analysis. It is what was identified as the method for elaboration of cases.

But, the essential aim of Lacan's interpretation of Freud's cases is to show how the singularity of a treatment can be transmitted, and thus be an epistemic value for other cases. Hence, he demonstrates the technical process in a psychoanalysis, its efficacy and at the same time the treatment deadlocks. After Lacan, Freud's cases demonstrate the structure-based clinic.

But what a subject formulates under transference leaves an irreducible space, which was partially there since the beginning of the experience. The subject proceeds via reordering contingencies from the past. Facts of history are newly construed. It is the elaboration of new myths which endeavor to capture the ultimate truth. There always remains a gap between new interpretations, and out of a symptom to what objects to signifier. It is the place of real. It forges itself as soon as the outset of analysis and the starting point is the subject's involvement. There is no chance to grab this real which is the real of singularity, without the analysand's involvement, but also without the analyst's involvement. At this point a question arises: what is a transmission in psychoanalysis?

That question has haunted the analysts and we should say fortunately. For when they become satisfied with their transmission, considering it as the good one, that will be when transmission begins to stagnate. There are signs of stagnating practices all along psychoanalysis history. It is along this thread that is taking shape the question of whether analysis always implies something being new, which eludes the norm; how do you transmit a singularity being by definition the exception? How do you convey the exception without deviating from an analytical clinic? On the other hand, what is the epistemic benefit to convey an exception, which by definition will not be recurring in other cases? Broadly speaking what is the use of a teaching when psychoanalysis aims toward singularity? The question is about the status of knowledge in psychoanalysis.

The case-based clinic exists precisely to thwart all preexisting knowledge. One may also notice that the case-based clinic is something else than the structure-based clinic. It does not exclude it, but it goes beyond. The clinic of structure aims to identify in the expressions of the unconscious what pertains to a specific clinical structure or to another one. The case-based clinic aims to singularity.

I resume the question about knowledge. I begin with the "Variations on the Standard Treatment" which is concomitant with Lacan's 1953 beginning of teaching. There, he criticizes the notion of "Variations", in so far as at the same time it refers to diversities of cases, and to variables there can be in a case. Lacan opposes a method, the ethical rigor, and puts forward: "without which [...], even if it is filled with psychoanalysis knowledge, can only amount to psychotherapy".[17] Here the question is: what is differentiating psychoanalysis from psychotherapies? And he sets out that: "psychoanalysis is not like any other form of therapeutics".[18] In that regard, he introduces an exigency he names "the theoretical formalization". Its relevance is due to the fact that it helps to differentiate it from the practical formalization. From a clinician's perspective this one consists in the quest to do well or not. Hence Lacan's first step is to put aside this question about doing well or not. It is in this text that Lacan is going to resume Freud's formulation which he makes use of as a foundation, and resumed several times in his teaching "cure as an added benefit of psychoanalytical treatment".[19]

It means that the analyst's concern does not primarily consist to heal but to analyze. So "cure as an added benefit", is a cure which will come as an effect of analysis. It means that Lacan denounces an abuse, which is the desire to heal. The analyst's desire is not a desire to heal. To become analyst, one has to have been at least healed from this desire, since it is a desire which stands upon a fantasy. In this text you observe Lacan evoking how by referencing to meta-psychological criteria, the analysts seek refuge in the clinic. There was a time, much later than 1953, when to refer to the clinic, the analysts were arguing that it was necessary to look for economical criterion, others were evoking topical criterion, or terms linked to meta-psychology, believing one could thus capture the essence of an analysis. If Lacan at that time was denouncing the analysts who were making use of meta-psychology to provide highbrow explanations, it was because it is a manner to formulate an inability to give a full account of what really happens in the analytical experiment. As Lacan said later in his "Discourse to psychiatrists", he denounced use of the theory consisting above all, and as a clinician to keep safe from any commitment.[20] He puts into perspective psychoanalytical knowledge when asserting: "any treatment, even if it is filled with psychoanalysis knowledge, can only amount to psychotherapy".[21]

In that regard, Lacan evokes a questionnaire that Edward Glover, a famous British analyst, had sent to the most distinguished analysts of the United Kingdom and which had led to a text published under the title *The Technique of Psychoanalysis.*[22] Glover mentions that the 63 analysts consulted to answer that questionnaire all agreed on one single item, that an analysis consists in analyzing the transference. On everything else, there were divergent views. While the purpose of the enquiry was an attempt to establish the therapeutical criteria of an analysis, the conclusion was that an eclecticism existed among practitioners. That led Lacan to consider that maintaining standards in analysis is based upon the interest of the analytic group. At that time the question already was the following one: what makes the guarantee of an analysis? Lacan was especially interested in the cause of the discord. I have been asking myself the following question: today if someone was questioning 63 distinguished analysts, what could they say about being Lacanian? Probably, you would have divergences too. *A fortiori*, divergences would be more pronounced if it were among all analysts, whole mingled Lacanian analytic communities. What, even back then, Lacan had denounced, was the dispersion that one notices as an effect of dispersion at the level of concepts. And it is not fortuitous in this 1953 text to find the idea of fundamental concepts. It's striking, we are in 1953 and more than ten years later Lacan holds his seminar, *The Four Fundamental Concepts of Psycho-Analysis*, right at the time when he is banned from the association about which, in 1953, he had denounced divergences in the transmission of psychoanalysis. He already had the idea that, to be able to step out of the deadlock attested by these divergences in analysis, one had to go through the reference to fundamental concepts. In other words, in 1953 Lacan establishes an inventory to make obvious how the analysts had been entangled in their practice, because of the absence of a conceptual compass. It seems paradoxical, that on the one hand Lacan denounces a use of concepts to keep safe from practice, and that on the other he advocates the recourse to fundamental concepts.

The paradox is only apparent. It disappears if one keeps in mind that the essential is the use one is having of concepts. There are good and bad uses. The good one is to suspend conceptualization when operating as analyst. The bad one is to make use of concepts to paste them to the case.

One may conclude that if the already acquired knowledge may become an obstacle to gather anything new in analytical experience, it does not exempt the analyst to formalize theoretically the experience he is confronted with. That is precisely where the clinic of real is. The question is dual: how in the clinic is it possible to affect the subject's real, but also how to transmit on the basis of the real of experience.

Passing through knowledge

Lacan wonders about "What the psychoanalyst must know".[23] It is a convergent question to what he enunciates at the same time in his seminar "However the subject who comes into analysis places himself, as such, in the position of someone who is in ignorance".[24] Without this position, adds Lacan, there is "no possible way" to experience. It is indeed one of the reasons for preliminary interviews. That is what you can find at the same time in another text, "The Function and Field of Speech and Language in

Psychoanalysis", where Lacan formulates differently: "the analyst's art must, on the contrary, involve suspending the subject's certainties until their final mirages have been consumed".[25] "Suspending the subject's certainties" or the subject's ignorance which is required from the outset, are going hand in hand. Indeed, if one follows this logic, one understands the reason why Lacan introduced some years later the dimension of transference as an assumption of knowledge. To have an assumption of knowledge, the analyst must make felt that the knowledge produced by the subject and his self-confidence are in fact myths overlaying the subject's being. So, there is a knowledge preceding the analysis, which falls in disuse, for it was just a screen. Then, there is to produce a knowledge; it is the pending knowledge in the symptom.

Thus, there is a fundamental dimension to make the subject feel ignorance, otherwise there is no assumption of knowledge. Ignorance as love and hate is a passion of the being. Very early, Lacan argues that ignorance is at the conjunction between symbolic and real. The fact that something's real indicates that it is an experience affecting the subject's being, which truly concerns him and which is uneasy to muster. To muster ignorance, one has to make symptom [*faire symptôme*]. Yet, is it so obvious for a subject to decide to change his relationship to ignorance?

Lacan evokes the subject's relationship with ignorance in terms of "*I don't want to know anything about it*"[26], by distinguishing the relationship to ignorance those who attend his seminar may have, and even Lacan's relationship to ignorance. To Lacan it is the opportunity to say that he is doing his seminar as an analysand and hence, being himself in position to analyze his "*I don't want to know anything about it*". It is also the opportunity to remind his audience that "it will be quite some time before you reach the same"[27] [*"d'ici que vous atteigniez le même il y aura une paye"*].

Here, the "*I don't want to know anything about it*", is less displayed as a negative passion than as the driving force towards a new relationship to ignorance. Lacan also connects the analysand's relationship to "*I don't want to know anything about it*" as linked to the end of analysis, for he poses that it appears when the analysand considers that his "*I don't want to know anything about it*" sounds enough to him.

Thus, throughout analysis there are things which change in the relationship to knowledge. Fundamentally what is changing is what is resisting to knowledge. Analysis is a practice which goes against the flow, namely not wanting to know. But Lacan two years later in his "Italian Note" goes further, when he poses a precise tipping point by the end of analysis as a moment of confluence with "the horror of knowledge" [*"l'horreur de savoir"*].[28]

What before was displayed as a progression towards knowledge, here is presented as a turning point. They are not two different proposals. The progression prepares the radical instant of confluence to the horror of knowledge. Therefore, the horror of knowledge has something to do with one's relationship with ignorance.

What is fundamental is that Lacan indicates an unprecedented desire, an effect of having been confronted to "the cause of his horror, of his own, his, detached from that of all the others, the horror of knowledge".[29]

That demonstrates the true transition from particular to singular. For what is essential is the singularity of the cause to the horror of knowledge, and how the analysand is facing it. But still, why does ignorance lie between symbolic and real? To situate ignorance on the symbolic side leaves a chance for the subject to modify his relationship to ignorance. Ignorance therefore, is not a pure passion coming out of real.

Lacan poses that what an analyst has to know is to ignore what he knows. It is not the same ignorance than the subject's, who is coming to the analysis. Hence, there is ignorance in someone who knows. It is the ignorance dealing with a knowledge, in the sense that an analyst knows that he cannot use it for another case, it is about an ethical choice. To ignore what he knows is precisely what presides over the analyst's silence. Likewise, when Lacan asserts that the analyst must ignore what he knows, it is a way to resume Freud's formulation under which each case has to be taken as a new one. Formulating it like this, one is on the side of the case-based clinic and not on the side of the structure-based clinic: when one says that one goes towards setting apart the difference from what makes a distinction, one goes against the pre-established knowledge. Thus, the analytical method goes against ignorance, the analyst's ignorance at the beginning, but above all the analysand's. Thereby, ignorance is at the beginning of the experience, for both of them, analysand and analyst.

In the same direction I put forward, Lacan, by referring to the analyst, asserts: "Indeed, the analyst cannot follow this path unless he recognizes in his own knowledge the symptom of his own ignorance".[30] It means that at the starting point, the analyst has to recognize that he himself is the symptom of an ignorance. From ignorance to what is happening to whomever is in front of him, but at the same time to him as well, he is present as an incarnation of this symptom of ignorance. He adds: "Ignorance must not, in fact, be understood here as an absence of knowledge"[31], then "non-knowledge, which is not a negation of knowledge but rather its most elaborate form".[32] It brings to life the idea that the situation of the analyst's non-knowledge is a condition of production of a knowledge. One finds in these formulations some precise backgrounds which prepare for the notion of "*I don't want to know anything about it*", as something causing the relationship to knowledge. That justifies the reference to the learned ignorance: "analysis cannot find its measure except along the pathways of a learned ignorance".[33]

It is why in his text "Variations on the Standard Treatment", Lacan is referring to the organization of training structures for psychoanalysis. Therefore, in 1953, one already sees the implicit reasons of his dissociation from IPA, which proceeds of a change of orientation from Lacan's part about the use of knowledge in psychoanalysis. It's what he always did. He taught and tried to transmit the analysis from his analysand's standpoint. Besides, each time one should apply it to oneself. Pre-digested knowledge is what is learnt in university.

He resumes these axes in his November 4th 1971 lesson "Knowledge of the Psychoanalyst", to indicate that ignorance far from being a deficit is linked to knowledge, and Lacan resumes the "learned ignorance". That was known since Nicolas de Cues wrote his *On Learned Ignorance*. What is new in Lacan's statement is what he poses about psychoanalysis, namely that it discloses an un-known knowledge, but which is on the subject's side. There precisely is a paradox, the subject reckons that he ignores, he may suppose the knowledge pertaining to the other, but what he does not perceive is that he already knew without knowing it.

In the "Proposition of 9 October 1967 on the Psychoanalyst of the School", Lacan argues that the analyst is "of the supposed knowledge he knows nothing".[34] Again, it is about the question of ignorance. Then he adds, "this in no way authorizes the psychoanalyst to be satisfied, knowing that he knows nothing, for what is at issue is what he has to come to know".[35] There, one enters into the analytical method, what there is to know.

Transmission and knowledge

When Lacan asserts that the analyst cannot satisfy himself knowing that he knows nothing, he is pushing forward two things. Firstly, the idea already his and not varying, is that at the outset of an analysis, the analyst ignores everything. Secondly, he cannot be satisfied with his own ignorance for there is a counterpart – what he has to know – and it concerns the structure. Yet what is crucial about the analytical method is what's next. What the analyst has to know "can be traced out upon the same relationship in reserve according to which all logic worthy of the name operates"[36] and a bit later, Lacan says "the un-known is arranged as the framework of knowledge".[37]

One realizes the possible consequences for the transmission of psychoanalysis. It cannot be based upon exhaustiveness in the demonstration, as science aims to, nor makes use of semblance of knowledge as does the academic discourse. To make possible a transmission, bearing in mind the analytic discourse, it has to take in consideration a real which founds psychoanalysis, which Lacan defines as "Psychoanalysis, what is it? It is the detection of the obscured, of what obscures the understanding, due to a signifier which tagged a point of the body".[38]

Therefore, it means, for each case to take the measure that the item to determine beyond the elucidation of desire, concerns a dimension which is partially non-transmissible. That is the reason why Lacan poses the unconscious as knowledge. The unconscious knowledge is what's coming later in

Lacan's elaborations, in lieu of what he had posed of the unconscious as the speaking truth. The un-known as frame of knowledge indicates that knowledge is on the unconscious side.

But there is also something non-transmittable, due to the fact that "truth is lying", or as he formulates it: "there is no truth that, in passing through awareness, does not lie".[39] In a case there is some unutterable. The unutterable is what a subject is unable to say, not because he is short of words, but because of the gap between the symbolic and the real.

Psychoanalysis is understood as a practice which always needs to be re-invented, but it demands that there be a demonstration on how a practice including the unconscious has effects on desire. That is a so-called analytical effect.

In this sense, in psychoanalysis, a case objects to pre-established knowledges in two different ways. By the subject's side, its elaboration is unique. By the analyst's side, there is objection insofar as the interpretation points towards the hole in knowledge. It should be noticed that in the clinic, the exception is an outlaw, in that sense it is a real. It is also one of Lacan's definitions for real: "the real is lawless".[40] I come to the point. The paradigm about what is transmitted out of a case is what is transmitted through the Pass. I shall expand on this point.

What appears as crucial and it is what is deduced from this mechanism, is the distinction between a transfer via elucubration and a transfer with effect of real. Lacan highlights the fact that a desire is not attested through the consistency of narrative told by the passand [le passant], but instead through the effect produced by the testimony and first and foremost onto the passers [les passeurs]. This effect, when it is obvious, is that of a conviction as clue of real.

It should be noticed as a fact of experience, that what matters in this effect of conviction is simultaneously what is said and what is not, thus a discontinuity between the "spoken words" [les dits]. In this sense, it is not because a testimony is extensive that it triggers the listener's conviction, but because between the meshes of a discourse, it makes felt the formulation of a desire.

One could object that a conviction is not linked to the real of a case, for it is always subjective. That's for sure. Except that, when it is shared by subjects with very different analytical experiences, it ceases to be subjective and then it constitutes a proof of real. That is also why Lacan sets two passers at the core of this mechanism, saying on the one hand: "From where then could an accurate testimony on whoever crosses this pass be expected, if not from another who, like him, is still this pass?"[41]; and on the other that they must be able to recognize in the passand the mark of the analyst's desire. Thus, the passer's conviction becomes crucial in the process which aims to recognize the emergence of this desire. Lacan makes orbiting around the passers' testimonies, the essence of the process of the pass.

But Lacan takes one more lap beyond conviction. It's the lap through affects. He highlights it with the *Witz*, the wit, in the pass. If efficient, it translates into a profit, the laugh. It is not linked to the other's castration but instead to a gain of satisfaction. Once more, it verifies itself if and only if, to the passand's satisfaction, it adds up the passers' satisfaction, and also to the satisfaction of the jury of the pass, and in doing so it attests that satisfaction is not an autistic affect. There is no satisfaction of the One without satisfaction of the others. In the case of the School, the passand's satisfaction echoes the community's satisfaction to which he belongs. It attests that a testimony succeeded in its analytical transmission.

One could add to this series of effects, conviction and satisfaction, the other's lightness. It is a feeling which is uneasy to obtain. In our practice, lightness is noticeable after a subject went through a complicated ordeal. The effect of lightness is also reflected in the analyst, and gives us the idea of what this affect may be by the end of analysis for the subject and the others. Lightness is the clue indicating that one has gone from tragedy to comedy.

In this sense, there should be made a distinction between result and effect. A result is transmitted from signifying logic. One may transmit how decreased the symptom is by the end of the analysis. By contrast, an effect may occur or not. It cannot be measured in advance, and it goes beyond consistency. Therefore, there is a surprise in the *Witz* of the end. Above all it is a surprise for who is telling it.

Its meaning does not consist to validate an affect from an effect of identification. For there is a dimension of possible identification produced by the resonance of case. Therefore, it is not about knowing if the case resonates with the proper analytical experience, but if the effect of analysis was produced through an original satisfaction.

Does it mean that the case model is the case which proves the success of a psychoanalysis? It would postulate a perfect model to exemplify a case. Yet, the case-based clinic does not imply purity of desire. It is what Lacan argued, asserting that the analyst's desire is not a pure desire. In the transmission of a case there is always a dimension which stays enigmatic. It is precisely why the mechanism of the pass includes a dimension of a bet. Failure should be considered in transmission of a case. That's happening when a case does not produce a desire on the jury's side of the pass. Clinic failures should be explored. That these failures exist does not mean that the saying of an analysis has not been seized. In this sense, there has been a case, even when something failed to be proved.

That the pass be a model to situate what a case is for psychoanalysis, must not turn the pass into some paralyzing ideal, nor to be considered as the only transmissible analytical clinic. However, the pass is a paradigm of what a clinical case is in psychoanalysis. Apart from cases of the pass, there exists an analytical clinic one may refer to, and that may be transmitted, provided that it be attempted to demonstrate how a case – including the analysand and the analyst – subverts what the theory, at some point in the history of psycho-analysis, sets as a *doxa*. In this sense, the case in analysis has an anti-*doxa* effect. It does not confirm the textual knowledge, instead it makes a hole in the consolidated knowledge.

In the "Introduction to a first volume of the *Écrits* (Walter Verlag)", Lacan moves around discourses, and formulates "For the question begins with there being types of symptoms, with there being a clinic. Only, there we have it: this is prior to analytic discourse".[42] So, the axis is not the meaning of symptoms but the fact that they order themselves.

"Types of symptoms" sends back to Freud's typical symptoms. A symptom is typical insofar as it enables to identify a clinical entity. Therefore, typical symptoms ordered the clinic preceding psychoanalysis. It is the clinic in the broad sense. The medical clinic already works to identify symptoms and the psychiatric clinic falls into this model. If one says "clinic", it is because it is a practice beside the sick person's bed.

Today the *evidence-based medicine* qualifies a new clinic, by supporting the fiction of an "a-theoretical" perspective which would legitimately impose itself by the mere fact of the strength of statistical figures. This new clinic is consistent with what different DSM[43] editions propose in psychiatry.

Let's proceed. Lacan said: "Nevertheless: it is before the analytic discourse, and if this one brings some light, it is sure but not certain."[44] Here Lacan emphasizes the clinical necessity to make use of discourses. You can be assured of what you collect as sign, but transmission is something else. The effective transmission provides evidence that the signs have been shared. For a case, to refer to the analytic discourse is what allows you to say if there has been an entry into this discourse, but also if there has been an exit. On the one hand should be distinguished the encounter with an analyst of the entry into the analytic discourse, on the other, should be distinguished the separation with an analyst of the exit from the analytic discourse. In this sense, the clinic of discourses becomes essential.

That is also what demonstrates the distinction between "to be sure" and "to be certain", as mentioned by Lacan. It corresponds to the distance between the intimate conviction and the demonstration. It is why Lacan delivers a discourse about one structure alone, Hysteria. Hysteria would be the only case of neurosis, where one can be sure and able to uplift it to the category of certainty.

One is self-confident, while to be certain implies a certainty being shared with others. One can be confident about what one collects as sign, its trans-mission is something else. The transmission displays evidence and becomes certainty. One could say that when one is certain, that is an anticipated cer-tainty needing to be confirmed. It should be noticed that Lacan handles things differently from Freud who tries to demonstrate the evidence about the unconscious as well. And Freud's choice is precisely what enables to attest it and to transmit it in the purest way, namely the obsessional neurosis.

That "pure" is what Freud highlights in the case designed as "the Wife and the Tablecloth". Freud demonstrates the effect of the unconscious in the formation of symptom and without the least recourse to the analyst's involvement.[45] He thus attempts to prove in the most complete way and without any possibility to consider it as an arbitrary hypothesis, that the existence of the unconscious is absolutely unrelated with the analytical interpretation.

Lacan poses:

> We need certitude because only it can be transmitted and demonstrated. This is the requirement of which history shows to our stupification that it was formulated well before science responded to it, and that even if the response had been other than the path clearing that the requirement produced, the condition from which it took its departure, the certitude that it was transmissible was satisfied there.[46]

The question is about the exigency to obtain a certitude within transmission. The logic had already aimed at the demonstration of certitude before science ever existed. Thus, the idea before science, was already to aim towards demonstration. Science has answered otherwise through an attempt to do a mathematics relying on nature, the aim being that the condition of transmissibility be satisfied.

Lacan with the *mathème* had already drawn a program for psychoanalysis which relies on the same condition of transmission, and I consider that the Borromean clinic answers to this same exigency.

In the same text, Lacan goes on: "We would have been wrong to pride ourselves on only putting it back there – were this with the reserve of the catch-as-catch-can." What is it one must not put back and what is meant by the "catch-as-catch-can"? I understand it like this: under the pretext that there exists contingency, we cannot abandon the use of logic in order to demonstrate the certainty.

So, on the one hand, Lacan poses that the aim to demonstrate must not be neglected. Simultaneously, he does not exclude the dimension of contingency. The "catch-as-catch-can" [*petit bonheur la chance*] refers to the previous page of the "Introduction to a first volume of the *Écrits*" about the "good hour" [*bon-heur*] and of the dimension of the encounter, which is always contingent. Regarding demonstration, Lacan does not neglect that there must be a part of contingency in what is of the order of transmission. It's shortly after, that it is emphasized: "For such opinion has for a long time given proof of being true, without all that constituting science (*cf. Meno* where it is a question of that) (*s'agite*)".[47]

What is evoked as being before science is Plato's *Meno*. Although there was no science, mathematics was already there and as a proof, Socrates, to help Meno to find a definition, suggests to make use of a mathematical method, that is the mathematical rationale. "To know what it is that virtue is like knowing what is a shape without any regard of it being a circle or a square".[48] To Lacan the reference to *Meno* is constant. Thus, very early he moves forward in his teaching, asserting as an answer to Jean Hypolite the following formulation:

> What we discover in analysis pertains to the level of *orthè doxa*. Everything which takes effect in the field of analytic action precedes the constitution of knowledge, which doesn't change the fact that in operating in this field we have constituted a knowledge and one which has even proved itself to be exceptionally efficacious, as is quite natural, since any science arises from a use of language which precedes its own constitution, and that it is through this use of language that the analytic action develops.[49]

In *Meno*, Socrates' opinion is that you only need to ask appropriate questions. One finds a method: already it is from non-knowledge that knowledge designs itself. Thus, Socrates resumes his discourse with Meno and together they conclude that since there is neither teachers nor pupils, virtue is not a science and cannot be taught. And continuing the dialogue, they agree that science is not the only way to guide human actions for the better, but there is also the true opinion. Hence, a true opinion posed like this is as valid as science.

On this point, one must revert to Lacan's statements in "L'Etourdit": "One cannot deny that there is here some progress on what remained to be questioned in the *Menon* about what is teachable".[50]

Therefore, barely nine months earlier, Lacan resumes the *mathème* to highlight what is not transmitted through verification. That is, what is not released through *mathème*.

What cannot be transmitted is tied to the undecidable and the undecidable is the real. From there, the role that Lacan assigns to the saying [*le dire*], the real of the saying [*du dire*] is therefore a conception of the transmission which aims to be as close as possible to demonstrating the indemonstrable.

It is Lacan's move in relation to *Meno* and it enables an understanding of the phrase in "Introduction...": "[in] *Meno* where it is a question of that" [qu'il *s'agite*]. *Meno* agitates himself to ensure that the true opinion be as valid as science, and Lacan demonstrates the existing gap between true opinion and science. This gap is about the real. True opinion agitates itself, for it is confronted to a move over the obstacle of the saying [*au dire*]. True opinion is truth in the real. The real is what prevents true opinion to become a saying [*un dire*]. Here what is told is the gap between truth and real.

Lacan adds:

> That clinical types arise from structure, this is what can already be written although not without wavering. This is only certain and transmissible

from the discourse of the hysteric. This is even how a real close to scientific discourse is manifested. One will remark that I have spoken of the real, and not of nature.[51]

Here Lacan resumes the notion of types of symptoms, rather than to use the clinical types. By formulating the idea of plural clinical types, he makes reference to the clinical structures. It resumes what Freud puts forward in his 17th conference:

"Typical" symptoms of an illness; they are approximately the same in all cases [...] But all these obsessional patients have a tendency to repeat, to make their performances rhythmical and to keep them isolated from other actions [...] In the same way, hysteria, in spite of its wealth of individual traits, has a superfluity of common, typical symptoms.[52]

And further: "And we must not forget that it is these typical symptoms, indeed, which give us our bearings when we make our diagnostic".[53]

Now, Lacan adds a different level, which is the clinical types. Clinical types fall under the ordering of symptoms. That is the medical process. One proceeds by ordering symptoms in clusters, trying to stay as close as possible to objectivation. It is interesting to notice that in the Geneva Conference, Lacan poses: "He would like us to listen, if I may say so, entirely independently of any knowledge we have acquired [...] This is very difficult because obviously the nature of experience is to prepare a pigeon-hole (de preparer un casier)".[54] Let me revert to "a real close to scientific discourse".[55] That enables us to pose a clinic of real. Again, the question is: what is certain and transmissible.

The formulation of scientific discourse is posed after the formalization of the four discourses. Thus, he proposes "in inscribing science at the register of hysteric discourse".[56] Then, in the same text, he asserts that: "science takes its *élans* from the discourse of the hysteric".[57] Further, barely two months after "Introduction to a first volume of the *Écrits*", Lacan participates in an interview which leads to the text "Television" and puts forward: "[they have] almost the same structure".[58] With this "almost", Lacan specifies immediately: "That is which explains our error, introduced by Freud himself, in hoping that one day there would be a thermodynamic able to provide – within the future of science – the unconscious with its posthumous explanation".[59]

The "knowledge" of science and the hysteric "knowledge" hold the same place: that of production. That being said, a fundamental difference parts them; the invention of the knowledge of science aims to figure out a knowledge "in the real", while the questioned knowledge in the hysteric's discourse, it is the knowledge already supposed in the Other. As Lacan said it in his conference in Milan in 1972: "that's the scientific approach. It is of course, to punctuate the world with mathematical signifiers... but to stop precisely at this... that this is to signify..."[60]

Lacan situates the emergence of the discourse of science, as a production of knowledge at the level of the hysteric's discourse, which challenges the master's authority. The hysteric does not give up in front of those who govern, nor in front of the church's authority. Hence, it promotes ideals of freedom, subjects' autonomy, possible *jouissances*. But science also produces a knowledge and tries to place it as a master. The hysteric's discourse, whose function is to produce desire, dissents from the master. The affinity of these two discourses is the finality, namely the production of knowledge. But the scientific discourse does not aim at the production of desire.

The discourse of science wants to ignore that the Other may be unfinished. It ignores what is the Other's void, where nestles the subject's truth, and the cause of his singular desire. Yet, if there actually exists a desire of the scientist, it does not spark any other desires, it aims to the mastery, the disappearance of the dimension of desire.

Let's come to Lacan's proposition "that the clinical types pertain to the structure, that's what already can be written not without fluctuation".[61] So, Lacan's option remains the structure. He does not say "pertain to the clinical structure"; saying that it pertains to the structure and admittedly it refers to the clinical structure, but also to the fact that the subject is structured by the language. In other words, there is a subject's particular structure depending on how he has been traversed by the language. I leave aside the proper modality of *jouissance* which is also the subject's structure, for it is mentioned in these lines.

Yet, where there is no fluctuation, it is because it can be written and transmitted. Therefore, it is valid only for hysterical structure, in so far as it is the only structure which may organize itself into a discourse. Depending on how the four discourses organize themselves, hysteria is the only one to fall in place as a discourse. If there remains any doubts on this question, you have to relate to what Lacan poses as the out-of-discourse [*hors discours*] of psychosis, or the need for the obsessional to hystericize in order to be able to step into analysis.

Yet, when Lacan says "This is only certain and transmissible from the discourse of the hysteric", I understand it like this: you have to have the structure of a discourse to transmit a clinical structure. It does not disqualify the certainty of a structure. One can be certain and unable to transmit it.

Let's now take the statement: "The real, it is not the nature".[62]

For a long time, different civilizations posed nature as real, even Lacan's definition of real as always coming over in the same place, pertains to this amalgam. Nature is immutable. It is the invariant. Yet, the discourse of science has hit the nature. With science, one moves from speech to writing in accordance to Galileo's statement: "Nature is written in mathematical language". We cannot but evoke here what Lacan later on puts forward in his teaching: "The real is lawless".[63] The real which has been invented by Lacan is not the real of science. It is a hazardous real, contingent in the fact that it lacks the natural law of the relationship between sexes. It is a hole inside the knowledge embodied in the real. It is a remain.

Notes

1 Lacan, J., "Le Séminaire, Livre XXV, Le moment de conclure", inédit, leçon du 15 novembre 1977. (My translation.)
2 Lacan, J., "Remarque sur le rapport de Daniel Lagache", in Écrits, Paris, Le Seuil, 1966, p. 684. ("Remarks on Daniel Lagache's Presentation: 'Psychoanalysis and Personality Structure'" in Écrits – Translation by Bruce Fink in collaboration with Héloïse Fink and Russell Grigg, p. 573.)
3 Lacan, J., "Le Séminaire, Livre XXV, Le moment de conclure", inédit, leçon du 15 novembre 1977. (My translation.)
4 Lacan, J., "Le Séminaire, Livre XXII, RSI", inédit, leçon du 18 février 1975. (The Seminar of Jacques Lacan, Book XX RSI, Seminar 6 Tuesday 18 February 1975, p. 111. Translation by C. Gallagher.)
5 Lacan, J., "Le Séminaire, Livre XXII, RSI", inédit, leçon du 18 février 1975. (The Seminar of Jacques Lacan, Book XX RSI, Seminar 6 Tuesday 18 February 1975, p. 111–112. Translation by C. Gallagher.)
6 Lacan, J., "Le Séminaire, Livre IX, L'Identification", inédit, séance du 21 février 1962.
7 Lacan, J., Le Séminaire, Livre XVI, d'Un Autre à l'autre, Paris, Le Seuil, 2006, pp. 299 and 310. ("The Seminar of Jacques Lacan, From an Other to the Other", p. 262. Translation by C. Gallagher.)
8 Lacan, J., "Introduction à l'édition allemande d'un premier volume des Écrits", in Autres écrits, Paris, Le Seuil, 2001, p. 557. ("Introduction to a first volume of the Écrits", Walter Verlag, published in Scilicet, 1975, n°5, pp. 11–17. Translation by J. W. Stone.)
9 Lacan, J., "Introduction à l'édition allemande d'un premier volume des Écrits", in Autres écrits, Paris, Le Seuil, 2001, p. 557. ("Introduction to a first volume of the Écrits", Walter Verlag, published in Scilicet, 1975, n°5, pp. 11–17. Translation by J. W. Stone.)
10 Alferi, P., Guillaume d'Ockham le singulier, Paris, Editions de Minuit, 1989, p. 5.
11 Lacan, J., "Introduction à l'édition allemande d'un premier volume des Écrits", in Autres écrits, Paris, Le Seuil, 2001, p. 557. Translation by J.W. Stone.
12 Lacan, J., "Introduction à l'édition allemande d'un premier volume des Écrits", in Autres écrits, Paris, Le Seuil, 2001, p. 557. Translation by J.W. Stone.
13 Lacan, J., "The Direction of the Treatment and the Principles of Its Power", in Écrits, p. 523. Translation by B. Fink.
14 Lacan, J., Le Séminaire, Livre VIII, Le Transfert, Paris, Le Seuil, 1991, p. 289. Translation by C. Gallagher.
15 Lacan, J., "L'Etourdit", in Autres écrits, Paris, Le Seuil, 2001, p. 473. Translation by C. Gallagher.
16 Lacan, J., "Radiophonie", in Autres écrits, Paris, Le Seuil, 2001, p. 415. Translation by J.W. Stone.
17 Lacan, J., "Variantes de la cure-type", in Écrits, Paris, Le Seuil, 1966, p. 324. ("Variations on the Standard Treatment", Écrits, New York and London, W.W. Norton and Company, 2002, p. 269. Translation by B. Fink in collaboration with H. Fink.)

18 Lacan, J., "Variantes de la cure-type", in Écrits, Paris, Le Seuil, 1966, p. 324. ("Variations on the Standard Treatment", Écrits, New York and London, W.W. Norton and Company, 2002, p. 269. Translation by B. Fink in collaboration with H. Fink.)

19 Lacan, J., "Variantes de la cure-type", in Écrits, Paris, Le Seuil, 1966, p. 324. ("Variations on the Standard Treatment", Écrits, New York and London, W.W. Norton and Company, 2002, p. 270. Translation by B. Fink in collaboration with H. Fink.)

20 Lacan gave a lecture known in France as "Petit discours aux psychiatres". Its full title is: Lacan J., "La psychanalyse et la formation du psychiatre », conférence du 10 novembre 1967, inédit.

21 Lacan, J., "Variantes de la cure-type", in Écrits, Paris, Le Seuil, 1966, p. 324. ("Variations on the Standard Treatment", Écrits, New York and London, W.W. Norton and Company, 2002, p. 269. Translation by B. Fink in collaboration with H. Fink.)

22 Glover, E., Technique de la psychanalyse, Paris, PUF, 1958. Translation by C. Laurin.

23 Glover, E., Technique de la psychanalyse, Paris, PUF, 1958, p. 349. Translation by C. Laurin,

24 Lacan, J., Le Séminaire, Livre I, Les écrits techniques de Freud, Paris, Le Seuil, 1975, p. 298. (The Seminar of Jacques Lacan: Book I: Freud's Papers on Technique. New York and London, W.W. Norton and Company, 1991, p. 271. Translation by J. Forrester.)

25 Lacan, J., "Fonction et champ de la parole et du langage en psychanalyse", in Écrits, Paris, Le Seuil, 1966, p. 324. ("The Function and Field of Speech and Language in Psychoanalysis", Écrits, New York and London, W.W. Norton and Company, 2002, p. 209. Translation by B. Fink in collaboration with H. Fink.)

26 Lacan, J., Le Séminaire, Livre XX, Encore, Paris, Le Seuil, 1975, p. 9. (The Seminar of Jacques Lacan, Book XX, Encore. Translation by C. Gallagher.) Emphasis in original.

27 Lacan, J., Le Séminaire, Livre XX, Encore, Paris, Le Seuil, 1975, p. 9. (The Seminar of Jacques Lacan, Book XX, Encore. Translation by C. Gallagher.)

28 Lacan, J., "Note Italienne", in Autres écrits, Paris, Le Seuil, 2001, p. 309. ("Italian Note". Translation by S. Schwartz.)

29 Lacan, J., "Note Italienne", in Autres écrits, Paris, Le Seuil, 2001, p. 309. ("Italian Note". Translation by S. Schwartz.)

30 Lacan, J., "Variantes de la cure-type", in Écrits, Paris, Le Seuil, 1966, p. 358. ("Variations on the Standard Treatment", Écrits, New York and London, W.W. Norton and Company, 2002, p. 297. Translation by B. Fink in collaboration with H. Fink.)

31 Lacan, J., "Variantes de la cure-type", in Écrits, Paris, Le Seuil, 1966, p. 358. ("Variations on the Standard Treatment", Écrits, New York and London, W.W. Norton and Company, 2002, p. 297. Translation by B. Fink in collaboration with H. Fink.)

32 Lacan, J., "Variantes de la cure-type", in Écrits, Paris, Le Seuil, 1966, p. 358. ("Variations on the Standard Treatment", Écrits, New York and London, W.W. Norton and Company, 2002, p. 297. Translation by B. Fink in collaboration with H. Fink.)

33 Lacan, J., "Variantes de la cure-type", in Écrits, Paris, Le Seuil, 1966, p. 358. ("Variations on the Standard Treatment", Écrits, New York and London, W.W. Norton and Company, 2002, p. 300. Translation by B. Fink in collaboration with H. Fink.)

34 Lacan, J., "Proposition du 9 octobre 1967 sur le psychanalyste de l'Ecole"crits, Paris, Le Seuil, 2001, p. 249. ("Proposition of 9 October 1967 on the Psychoanalyst of the School", p. 6. Translation by R. Grigg.)

35 Lacan, J., "Proposition du 9 octobre 1967 sur le psychanalyste de l'Ecole"crits, Paris, Le Seuil, 2001, p. 249. ("Proposition of 9 October 1967 on the Psychoanalyst of the School", p. 6. Translation by R. Grigg.)

36 Lacan, J., "Proposition du 9 octobre 1967 sur le psychanalyste de l'Ecole", in Autres écrits, Paris, Le Seuil, 2001, p. 249. ("Proposition of 9 October 1967 on the Psychoanalyst of the School", p. 6. Translation by R. Grigg.)

37 Lacan, J., "Proposition du 9 octobre 1967 sur le psychanalyste de l'Ecole", in Autres écrits, Paris, Le Seuil, 2001, p. 249. ("Proposition of 9 October 1967 on the Psychoanalyst of the School", p. 6. Translation by R. Grigg.)

38 Lacan, J., Le Séminaire, Livre XIX, Le savoir du psychanalyste, inédit, leçon du 4 mai 1972. (My translation.)

39 Lacan, J., "Préface à l'édition anglaise du Séminaire XI", in Autres écrits, Paris, Le Seuil, 2001, p. 571. ("Preface to the English-Language Edition – Seminar XI". Translation by A. Sheridan.)

40 Lacan, J., Le Séminaire, Livre XXIII, Le sinthôme, Paris, Le Seuil, 2005, p. 137. (The Seminar of Jacques Lacan: Book XXIII: The Sinthome, p. 118. Translation by A.R. Price.)

41 Lacan, J., "Proposition du 9 octobre 1967 sur le psychanalyste de l'Ecole", in Autres écrits, Paris, Le Seuil, 2001, p. 249. ("Proposition of 9 Octobre 1967 on the Psychoanalyst of the School", p. 10. Translation by R. Grigg.)

42 Lacan, J., Introduction a L'edition Allemande Des Écrit, Scilicet, 1975, n°5, pp. 11–17. "Introduction to a first volume of the Ecrits (Walter Verlag)" Scilicet, 1975, n°5, p. 5. Translated by Jack W. Stone.

43 Diagnostic and Statistical Manual.

44 Lacan, J., Introduction a L'edition Allemande Des Écrit, Scilicet, 1975, n°5, pp. 11–17. "Introduction to a first volume of the Ecrits (Walter Verlag)" Scilicet, 1975, n°5, p. 5. Translated by Jack W. Stone.

45 Freud, S., "Le sens des symptômes" (17è conférence), in Conférences d'introduction à la psychanalyse, Paris, Gallimard, 1999, pp. 329–348. ("The Sense of Symptoms" (XVII), in Introductory Lectures on Psychoanalysis, W.W. Norton and Company, 1977, pp. 285–304.)

46 Lacan, J., "Introduction à l'édition allemande d'un premier volume des Écrits", in Autres écrits, Paris, Le Seuil, 2001, p. 557. ("Introduction to a first volume of the Écrits", Walter Verlag, published in Scilicet, 1975, n°5, pp. 11–17. Translation by J. W. Stone.)

47 In the French text, the expression "qu'il s'agite" is used, meaning to agitate oneself. It is a pun, indeed there are two words which are euphonically very close, namely: "il s'agit" (without an e) and "il s'agite" (with an e), the first one means "it comes to" and the second one means "to agitate oneself".

48 Plato, Menon, Paris, Flammarion, 1999.

49 Lacan, J., Le Séminaire, Livre II, Le moi dans la théorie de Freud et dans la technique de la psychanalyse, Paris, Le Seuil, 1978, p. 30. ("The Seminar of Jacques Lacan: Book II: Ego in Freud's Theory and in the Technique of Psychoanalysis", W.W. Norton, New York and London, 1991, p. 19. Translated by Sylvana Tomaselli with Notes by J. Forrester.)

50 Lacan, J., "L'Etourdit", in Autres écrits, Paris, Le Seuil, 2001, p. 481. ("L'Etourdit". Translation by C. Gallagher.)

51 Lacan, J., "Introduction à l'édition allemande d'un premier volume des Écrits », in Autres écrits, Paris, Le Seuil, 2001, p. 557. ("Introduction to a first volume of the Écrits", Walter Verlag, published in Scilicet, 1975, n°5, pp. 11–17. Translation by J. W. Stone.)

52 Freud, S., "Le sens des symptômes" (17è conférence), in Conférences d'introduction à la psychanalyse, Paris, Gallimard, 1999, pp. 346–347. ("The Sense of Symptoms" (XVII), Introductory Lectures on Psychoanalysis, W.W. Norton and Company, 1977, pp. 301–302.)

53 Freud, S., "Le sens des symptômes" (17è conférence), in Conférences d'introduc-
    tion à la psychanalyse, Paris, Gallimard, 1999, pp. 346–347. ("The Sense of
    Symptoms" (XVII), Introductory Lectures on Psychoanalysis, W.W. Norton and
    Company, 1977, pp. 301–302.).
54 Lacan, J., "Conférence de Genève sur le symptôme" Le Bloc-notes de la psycha-
    nalyse, n°5, 1985, p. 5–23. ("Geneva lectures on the Symptom", p. 11. Translation
    by R. Grigg.)
55 Lacan, J., "L'Etourdit", in Autres écrits, Paris, Le Seuil, 2001, p. 481. ("L'Etour-
    dit". Translation by C. Gallagher.)
56 Lacan, J., "Radiophonie", in Autres écrits, Paris, Le Seuil, 2001, p. 431. Transla-
    tion by J.W. Stone.
57 Lacan, J., "Radiophonie", in Autres écrits, Paris, Le Seuil, 2001, p. 436. Transla-
    tion by J.W. Stone.
58 Lacan, J., "Télévision", in Autres écrits, Paris, Le Seuil, p. 541. ("Television: A Chal-
    lenge to the Psychoanalysis Establishment", New York and London, W.W. Norton,
    1990, p. 19. Translation by J. Mehlman.)
59 Lacan, J., "Télévision", in Autres écrits, Paris, Le Seuil, p. 541. ("Television: A Chal-
    lenge to the Psychoanalysis Establishment", New York and London, W.W. Norton,
    1990, p. 19. Translation by J. Mehlman.)
60 Lacan, J., "Discours de Jacques Lacan à l'Université de Milan le 12 mai, 1972", in
    Lacan in Italia 1953–1978, Milan, La Salamandra, 1978, pp. 32–35. ("Discourse
    of Jacques Lacan at the University of Milan on May 12, 1972 [The Capitalist
    Discourse] p. 16. Translation by J.W. Stone.)
61 Lacan, J., "Discours de Jacques Lacan à l'Université de Milan le 12 mai, 1972", in
    Lacan in Italia 1953–1978, Milan, La Salamandra, 1978, pp. 32–35. ("Discourse
    of Jacques Lacan at the University of Milan on May 12, 1972 [The Capitalist
    Discourse] p. 16. My translation.)
62 Lacan, J., "Discours de Jacques Lacan à l'Université de Milan le 12 mai, 1972", in
    Lacan in Italia 1953–1978, Milan, La Salamandra, 1978, pp. 32–35. ("Discourse
    of Jacques Lacan at the University of Milan on May 12, 1972 [The Capitalist
    Discourse] p. 16. My translation.)
63 Lacan, J., Le Séminaire, Livre XXIII, Le sinthôme, Paris, Le Seuil, 1999, p. 137.
    ("The Seminar of Jacques Lacan: Book XXIII: The Sinthome", Polity Press,
    Cambridge, 2016, p. 118. Translation by A.R. Price.)

Chapter 2

The Unconscious Knowledge

And the Original Symptom

The learned ignorance

In "Crucial Problems for Psychoanalysis", Lacan demonstrates how by the means of the introduction to a new dimension, the signifier, psychoanalysis would allow to expand the knowledge to the whole field of symptoms in psychiatry. Indeed, Lacan poses that "there is to know" about the symptom.[1]

Thus, he connects knowledge and analytical symptom, and asserts that "The category of knowledge is precisely where is lying what is radically allowing us to perceive the function of the symptom".[2] It is this connection which leads him to this formulation: "there is always in the symptom the indication that there is a question of knowledge [...] in neurosis it is implied, given, in the original symptom that the subject has not come to know".[3]

Already let's notice that, by evoking the original symptom, Lacan introduces a necessity, that of differentiating the original symptom, the one linked to the answer to infantile trauma, from the other formations of compromises, symptomatic, which forge themselves out of this original symptom, and which are either its metonymy or a substitution. The original symptom is the tissue onto which rests the subject's singularity. What's essential is that it traces a perspective starting from the distinction between knowledge and learning. To know one's symptom, in the sense of knowing oneself, falls under what we've learned as pertaining to the ego's register. Lacan formulates it like this: "Man knows more than he thinks to. But the substance of this knowledge, the materiality which is beneath, is nothing more than the signifier as having effects of significance".[4]

This surplus of knowledge refers to the unconscious, and this indication from Lacan coming by the end of his teachings is straight in the logic he poses earlier, about a knowledge the subject believes he is not having at his disposal. We'll come to this.

At the same time, there is what the analyst must know: Lacan is very clear when he says that the analyst is not an ordinary man. That is to say, that he sets himself apart through a use of the speech which is out of everyone's reach. Therefore, the difference between the analyst and somebody else is not

DOI: 10.4324/9781003568315-3

only a difference of experience. The difference is about the use of speech. But it must be nuanced. When Lacan says that the analyst must ignore what he knows, that does not mean that he has to satisfy himself with "I know nothing". There is a know-how of the use of speech, and about it there is a demand exerting a strain onto the analyst. Thus, when one says that the analyst must ignore what he knows, it concerns the outset of the experience. Indeed, what does he know about the other's unconscious? At the outset of an analysis, he knows nothing in particular about a subject. To pretend to know, whereas one does not know, is in analysis the other name for resistance. That is what Lacan puts forward with the famous formulation: "there is no other resistance in analysis than that of the analyst".[5] But what is exactly this resistance? One finds it each time, and all along the analysis, when the analyst makes use of a knowledge which does not come from the analysand's unconscious. It is only with regard to a master's knowledge that there is a resistance. This is also the attitude withheld by Lacan to set up his seminar, to deliver a discourse which makes a hole into the existing [en place] knowledge. What it means, either in the teacher's position when it comes to psychoanalysis or in the analyst's position, is to go against the comfort provided by learned knowledge. To say that one sets up a seminar as an analysand, means to set up a seminar from a position of a divided subject. It would be to intend to say something and then perceiving that what is said does not coincide with the original idea. It does not mean to follow a program where everything is traced beforehand. It means to give oneself the possibility of being surprised, by the situation, by the audience, by oneself. It is what yields the conditions to capture another "spoken word" [un dit] out of oneself and it matches with the analysand's position.

Consequently, it could seem odd to use the term of *subject supposed-to-know* to designate the transference. The assumption of knowledge is very specific; it is not an assumption which focuses on the order of the world. It tells the difference between knowledge and learning [connaissance]. The supposed knowledge, to the analyst, concerns the proper knowledge of the unconscious; it is why Lacan posed that unconscious is knowledge. Long after having said that the unconscious is the speaking truth, Lacan poses the unconscious as knowledge.

The unconscious knowledge is a thesis that one finds from the outset when Lacan poses: "The unconscious is the chapter of my history that is marked by a blank or occupied by a lie: it is the censored chapter".[6] It is a chapter that cannot be read without analysis, but which is written. It is precisely there, that lies the assumption of knowledge. And for the analysand, the preliminary interviews are used to establish the analyst as the partner to whom the subject supposes the knowledge in order to decipher the unconscious enigma. Therefore, we should already underline that the assumption of knowledge is something else than the assumption of learning [la connaissance]. One supposes learning [la connaissance] for scientists, educators, and physicians. The specificity of a subject in analysis is to suppose the unconscious knowledge to the analyst.

Several of Lacan's formulations prepare that of the unconscious as being a knowledge. For instance, in the same text, Lacan refers to hieroglyphs of the symptom of hysteria, as the body's hieroglyphs. It already poses the idea that there exists for the subject some unknown enigmas, that they are inscriptions in the body, and that they must be deciphered through the interpretation of the unconscious. Therefore, the formulation "Hieroglyphics of hysteria"[7] already contains the notion that there exists for the subject some inscriptions in the body, written in an unknown language. Then a partner able to read them has to be found. In this sense, analysis is an experiment of translation. In another language, what is writing itself in the unconscious, because of repression, has to be translated into a familiar language, accessible to the subject. It is all the same, when one says "censored chapter". A censorship consists to make illegible a sentence or an image. The analyst, through the process of free association he sets up, is supposed to restore the legibility. In this sense, analysis is a reading practice focused onto a hidden text.

Let's resume the preliminary interviews, and make use of them to bring out the subject's relationship to the unconscious, that is something else than to circumscribe them to the diagnostic. Diagnostic in psychoanalysis raises the question of "what for?" Indeed, for the analyst it's acting as a benchmark, it is an anticipation of a singular knowledge which may be brought out during the treatment, but at the same time it is double-edged. A diagnostic is a knowledge in support of a prevision, with the risk of any approach sustaining itself upon a prevision, that of not leaving an open door to the unexpected. In other words, the risk is that the treatment induces the confirmation of the prevision. Therefore, it is a complex question. There is on the one hand what the analyst has to be informed with, for instance the repetition of any passages to the act [*passages à l'acte*]. They constitute indicators of the future of an analysis. With the prevision, one reduces the ignorance one may have about the analysand. But at the same time, the prevision should not hinder the essence of the analytical clinic, the surprises of desire. It's noteworthy in the practice of control. The analyst who conveys a case is waiting for the attestation of a diagnostic, and most often one understands that he is expecting a case of neurosis. Why this preference? Because, one presumes with the neurotic subject a much better aptitude to the effects of analysis. One understands here, that this use of diagnostic is an obstacle to the case-based clinic. The case-based clinic is different from the clinic resting on the diagnostic. The diagnostic method is in support of the anticipation; it is the medical method the psychiatric clinic made use of. This is a method which makes use of experience. Indeed, the diagnostic fulfils what the analyst does not know. It fulfils the lack-of-knowledge [*manque-à-savoir*] from what can be perceived. It is the misuse of diagnostic. The misuse is to believe that one captures what is going on for a subject, once one poses the diagnostic.

Diagnostic in psychoanalysis comes under a clinic which organizes the experience out of the structure. Yet, what one must realize is that knowledge over the structure turns out to be insufficient to organize the analytical experience. There certainly exists an exigency weighing upon the analyst, that of a knowledge upon the structure, and it is why he cannot satisfy himself by knowing nothing. At the same time the analyst must know that diagnostic alone is not the only guidance to analytical experience. I shall develop these two points, structure and case.

Knowledge about the structure concerns a clinic which aims to capture the common denominator. How does one usually proceed? Most often, by detecting the clinical structure, one tries to determine how phenomena seemingly very dissimilar contain a core, which would be identical for all. Perforce, to capture the common denominator, one implements them in series. That is to say, one picks up a case, one attempts to exclude the psychotic phenomena, then one compares it – for instance, if one is in an obsessional neurosis to the other obsessional cases, one tries to confront it to cases of hysteria, then one relates it to the Rat Man's case. If it matches regarding the fundamental core, one concludes that it is an obsessional neurosis. That is what Lacan suggested when he evoked the fundamental symptom of doubt. It means that it should be identifiable in each case of obsessional neurosis. It is what I call the fundamental core, it is the fact of the prevalence of a symptom, as an answer to what is foreclosed in the unconscious, in this case, the signifier of death.

One applies this process *mutatis mutandis* to hysteria, with the slight difference that the fundamental symptom concerns the attempt to grasp the sexual belonging, as an answer to the signifier of the foreclosed sexual difference in the unconscious.

Indeed, it enables identification of the answer produced by a subject in his structure to the missing signifier in the unconscious. Because, for all subjects, there exists in the unconscious a foreclosed signifier. And the structure is the answer to this hole in the unconscious. Therefore, a diagnostic enables to know the answer given by a structure of language, precisely at the weak spot of the grip of language over the body, which leaves a hole in the unconscious. However, it is insufficient to outline what organizes the analyst's practice. Here precisely, I come to the second point.

What more essentially is leading the analytical experience? In that regard, I resume the subject supposed of knowledge, as a pivot around which the experience of analysis organizes itself. In that sense Lacan gives it an essential role in his "Proposition of 9 October 1967 on the Psychoanalyst of the School". In this text Lacan reverts to the non-knowing question. Before getting there, Lacan's distinction of the analytical situation concerns both analysand and analyst. Yet, Lacan says: "if psychoanalysis consists in maintaining an agreed-upon situation between two partners, who place themselves there as psychoanalysand and psychoanalyst, it can only unfold by the third constituent".[8] Therefore, between both partners, analysand and analyst, Lacan inserts a third one. It is a "third constituent which is the signifier introduced into the discourse that thereby establishes itself, and which has a name: the supposed subject of knowledge".[9] Hence, that third one supposes the introduction of a signifier and the discourse which institutes itself. It clearly indicates that the analyst is not exactly the supposed subject of knowledge, but he who brings it into being. In other words, there is the analysand, the analyst, and between them, the supposed subject of knowledge. One may notice that Lacan's endeavor consists in encompassing – and it's fundamental – what sets the analysis in motion. There, he refers to a situation which could not develop without the third one.

Here, the aftermath is of interest. Lacan introduces the idea of a discourse establishing itself out of it [*qui s'en instaure*]. We are in 1967, more than two years before the formalization of four discourses in *The Other Side of Psychoanalysis*, and already we find the premises of what is the entry into the analytic discourse, since Lacan makes use of the expression of an "established discourse". An "established discourse" means "a discourse which was not there"; it is established because of the supposed subject-supposed-to-know [*le sujet-supposé-savoir*]. With the "established discourse", we see a change of clinic. We move from a clinic of detection inside a discourse to a clinic of discourses, such as it may emerge from *The Other Side of Psychoanalysis*. For the analysand it is much less a dialectic detection, than a change of discourse at the outset of analysis, and then all along the psychoanalytical experience.

Over all, the clinic of discourse is the transition from a discourse to another one. At the outset of analysis, it is the entry into the hysterical discourse, then its passage to the analytic discourse. For the analyst, the clinic of discourse consists as well to avoid the academic discourse or the master's discourse. Therefore, at the same time the clinic of discourse concerns the analysand and the analyst. Both are caught in a discourse with this specificity of the analytic discourse, namely that it depends on the analyst's handling of "object *a*". In this sense, it can be argued that what founds the clinic of discourses is the analyst's capacity, during the treatment, to handle "object *a*". Thus, the responsibility for creating conditions of a discursive change, falls to the analyst. Already in "Proposition of 9 October 1967 on the Psychoanalyst of the School", Lacan resumes the term of *discourse* as he used it before in its common sense. A discourse is quite simply someone's statements, but at the same time and from a linguistic perspective, it is also the language being put into action and assumed by the speaking subject [*le sujet parlant*]. That is something else than to speak [*parler*]. To say something is insufficient to be in a discourse. It must be noticed that as well as arguing in this text "the discourse which establishes itself", Lacan also formulates "the signifier introduced". It indicates the need for something new, as being a condition to step in analysis, and it anticipates the idea that in an analytic discourse, it is the analyst who acts as an agent who determines the discourse.

But it is in *The Other Side of Psychoanalysis* that the clinic of discourses takes shape with the idea that the analyst establishes the semblance of "object *a*". It gives the idea that for the analytic discourse to be set up, there has to be someone who assumes the function. Unlike the other discourses where a subject and his partner are caught in a discourse, in the analytic one, it is one of them, the analyst, who sets it up. Therefore, it is the analyst who is in charge of the analytic discourse. It weighs on him to create the conditions for the hysteric discourse to switch to the analytic discourse, and throughout the treatment to use it as the medium.

Then Lacan moves to the analyst's relationship with the subject-supposed-to-know [*le sujet-supposé-savoir*], and poses that "the analyst of the supposed knowledge, he knows nothing". There again, is the question about ignorance, then he adds: "This in no way authorizes the psychoanalyst to be satisfied in the knowledge that he knows nothing, for what is at issue is what he has to come to know".[10] Here precisely, I think that one accesses the meaning of the case-based clinic. The case-based clinic is a clinic of the un-known [*non-su*], which traces the production of a knowledge as a perspective of the future. Are we going to get access to it or not? Neither the analysand nor the analyst knows it. It is another way to resume Lacan's idea when he says, that it does not mean to understand. And non-understanding [*ne-pas-comprendre*] means to distrust the experience one has about the words. Hence, the un-known [*non-su*] is in the same perspective, that of the non-understanding [*le ne-pas-comprendre*], and it is a clinical position which differs from empathy. Empathy means "I can put myself in lieu of you". Empathy is based upon experience. Yet the analyst, when he bases himself upon his own experience as a subject or as an analysand, puts himself in lieu of the other. On the contrary the un-known starts from "I understand nothing". Maybe it is at the end of an analysis that the analyst understands something.

One must not confound the un-known as the analyst's ethical position, and a condition to move towards knowledge with the semblance of the analyst. Semblance supposes to indicate simultaneously that the analysand has to produce a knowledge and that the analyst has to yield signs showing he has a knowledge at his disposal. Otherwise, the risk for the analysand would be the dismissal of the supposed subject of knowledge, and so before the analytical operation would be finalized. Along the same lines, the un-known [*le non-su*] may sometimes produce a negative transference, which is an effect of the de-supposition of knowledge [*la désupposition du savoir*]. Therefore, the analyst's un-know [*non-su*], nevertheless needs a dimension of semblance on the analyst side. Let's notice the transferential phenomenon which pops up when the semblance of "object *a*" tumbles before the end of the analysis.

It is the analysand who dismisses the analyst: "Ah! You don't understand, it means that you don't know while you should know!" There is a nuance which needs to be perceived between the negative transference, and the end of analysis. In both cases, there is a dismissal of the analyst's supposed knowledge. The difference lies in the last part of the sentence: "you should know". In the case of negative transference, it means that the analysand does not suppose, or no longer supposes, the knowledge of this one-analyst [*cet analyste-là*]. If the phenomenon persists, it is an analytical impasse, and often the outcome is to resume the analysis with another analyst. If the analysand is at the end of his analysis, the de-supposition [*la désupposition*] of knowledge in regard of the analyst combines itself with the conviction of a "that's enough" about the request to decipher the unconscious.

Therefore, this is not easy for the analyst to set about a semblance of "object *a*", enabling the emergence of a subject-supposed-to-know [*le sujet-supposé-savoir*], and at the same time, sustain himself with an un-known [*non-su*] position. However, why did Lacan enhance the non-knowledge as such as to make it fill a paramount place, that of giving a frame to knowledge? This term of *frame* is interesting because it sends back to the standards of the IPA. The protocol – what has been called the *setting*: the schedules, the waiting-room, the way appointments are organized – for the IPA, it is the frame. Yet, the fact that Lacan says that it is the non-knowledge [*le non-savoir*] which gives the frame of knowledge, is because non-knowledge [*non-savoir*] is the condition for a knowledge nested inside the unconscious to emerge. That is the reason why Lacan poses the unconscious as knowledge. The un-known as framework of knowledge, it poses that there exists only one frame in analysis, that which is given through knowledge being on the unconscious side. From this assertion, the whole question is: how possible is an operation which does not start from a pre-existing knowledge, but which produces a knowledge being a function of truth for a subject? That is what Lacan is going to pose as the analytic discourse, knowledge instead of truth, which conditions in analysis the function of interpretation. Therefore, the analyst does not have to understand, he has to interpret.

The informed desire

In the "Proposition of 9 October 1967 on the Psychoanalyst of the School", Lacan establishes a distinction between "the vacuity of incompetence" and "the non-marked of naivety",[11] and articulates them to ignorance and non-knowledge. Furthermore, Lacan will use that same term of naivety when talking about the mechanism of the pass he refers to the passer [*le passeur*], who is in the situation to transmit the passand's [*le passant*] testimony. Lacan assigns to the passer this position of naivety. This conflicts with the "I have understood, that's enough". Naivety instead, while having understood something, serves to make the interlocutor believe that one has not fully understood, and this in order to push him to explain further. The analyst's naivety urges the analysand to add an "extra-spoken word" [*un dit de plus*]. Hence, naivety matches the analyst's position, besides it's synonym of ingenuity. *Ingenuity* or *naivety*, these terms proceed against chronicity, which is the moment when in the experience, one is not anymore surprised by oneself. Naivety is a way to ignore experience. That is: each time one restarts and tries to see, and it is what creates out of an analysis the conditions to make an original experience.

Naivety is also a position of semblance. As well, that means saying to the other that one has not understood, whereas one has fully understood. "The vacuity of incompetence" as evoked in this context by Lacan, is the fact that one does not know, while one is supposed to know. When one says about someone that he is an incompetent, it is because he is supposed to know something. The vacuity is the non-knowing [*non savoir*], whereas one should know. The analysand who heads towards the analyst to tell him "You are a failure", is actually telling him "If I go astray, it's because of you".

Basically, what makes the difference between the naive and the failure? The naive is someone who asks the question nobody asks, either because one has a sense of decency for asking it, or because one is afraid to be considered as someone stupid. Well, you have to dare to appear as a stupid analyst: "Is that so, it's like this for you?" Therefore, when someone is willing to ask a stupid question, there, one detects naivety.

Naivety is also the opposite of being comfortably installed in the academic discourse or in the master's one. In the academic discourse, knowledge is standing for semblance and is the agent of discourse, it makes objection to naivety. What is controlling this discourse is not the question addressed to the other, instead it falls under a "ask me some questions, I have the answers". As well, for the master's discourse which requires that a signifier S1 assumes the control of the discourse; it is the opposite of naivety. A master never considers himself as being naive. Someone who never asks any questions, one can be sure that he is comfortably installed in a position where he believes that he has settled his relationship with naivety, or that he fears the other's judgement.

Let us take the example of an exile. He asks the question that no one does. While for all of us, there are things which are obvious, the exile will interrogate them. He points out what is not straightforward, while it is about what is accepted by the others. It compels us to go back to the explanation. For an exile there would be a will to know which creates an affinity with the naive. It is the reason why, for the analyst, the exile holds an appropriate position.

One may notice the importance of Lacan's proposition: "analysis cannot find its measure except along pathways of a learned ignorance".[12] The learned ignorance puts us in the perspective of an analysis whereby one progresses from non-knowledge to knowledge. Yet, to progress within knowledge is something else than to progress within learning [*la connaissance*].

It is appropriate to consider this other dimension, namely that there is a correlation between the analyst's naivety and the informed desire. In *The Ethics of Psychoanalysis*, Lacan refers to the analyst's desire as being an informed desire.[13] Above all, the analyst must be informed to not understand too quickly. In that sense the informed desire needs naivety.

Let's resume the difference between learning [*la connaissance*] and knowledge. Most often in English, knowledge is the usual word either for learning or knowledge. For Lacan the differentiation is: knowledge *a minima*, is identified as being an S2, a signifier adding itself to a first signifier. That introduces a differentiation between what is said and what is heard of what is said.

That is to say, that someone may be perfectly speaking, be within the language, and that language be a series of S1. The S2 introduces a second level, it introduces a meaning to what has been said until then. That is precisely the question of knowledge, to introduce a new signifier. For you may be perfectly in the series of S1 and be within learning [*la connaissance*] and not within knowledge.

Let's take the case of autism. All that an autist can say is a learning [*connaissance*] of S1, is not a learning [*connaissance*] of S2. S1 learning [*connaissance*] indicates that a series of terms may join one after the other but without the last term, the S2, which gives a meaning to the whole. Therefore is missing the signifier of knowledge, while there are signifiers of learning [*la connaissance*]. Knowledge as S2 is linked to the unconscious. When you are within the learning [*la connaissance*], you are within the register of the self. When one moves to the unconscious register, there is the possibility to produce some S2.

I am coming to the informed desire. Lacan made use of the term *informed* well before having posed the analyst's desire as an informed desire. Thereby, for psychosis he uses the expression "the informed subject" with reference to Schreber, and to designate the subject's relationship to the signs of the unconscious.

That justifies a detour through psychosis. To be informed gives the indication that you have noticed something. It is interesting in terms of clinic. It provides a compass which orientates the subject throughout his life, and constitutes a fundamental tool acting as a manual about what may be promoted in the psychoanalytical treatment of a psychotic subject. One could support the idea that in psychosis, and as far as possible, the treatment is about to produce an informed subject. Informed of what? For example, a subject being informed of situations which can determine a trigger. It gives an indication of a know-how as well as the favorable conditions to avoid this trigger or to avoid its recurrence. A psychotic subject who has been through numerous contingencies may be able to identify the common denominator of these experiences, and therefore be informed for a next time.

The informed subject is also a subject who knows what he must not be confronted by, he must know what he has to say no to, ultimately what to choose between a certain position or another. In the Lacanian clinic, we insist on underlining that in the transference in psychosis, the analyst's position consists in occupying the place of the "secretary of the insane". Although that expression is appropriate to indicate the analyst's place in the treatment of the psychotic subject, it does not say what could be its purpose. With the notion of "informed subject", we are in line with what can be expected in the analysis of psychosis. Nevertheless, with this proposition we do not evoke a singularity. Instead, it indicates what can usually be proposed in the treatment of a psychotic subject. There still is an effort to be made in the case-based clinic.

We measure the gap between a clinic of subject aiming to "be informed" through one's unconscious, and a clinic of the singularity which aims for an access to a know-how concerning what he perceives as a dis-accommodation [désaccommodation] of his being in the world. This unique know-how, it comes apart from all the others.

It would be interesting to examine Lacan's other formulations, enabling in psychosis the definition of the subject's relationship to the unconscious. In Lacanian-inspired psychoanalysis, we often insist on the expression "the open-air unconscious" [l'inconscient à ciel ouvert]. It indicates an unsubscribe [désabonnement] from the unconscious, an effect of the non-process of repression. Yet, even if the expression is right, it neglects Lacan's other comments about the unconscious in a psychosis. Hence, in terms of structure, it indicates explicitly: "Freud sees as the subjective connotations of the unconscious when recognized – that the delusion deploys its whole tapestry around the power of creation attributed to the words of which the divine rays (Gottesstrahlem) are the hypostasis".[14] Then he adds: "Divination by the unconscious no doubt warned the subject very early on that, unable to be the phallus the mother is missing, there remained the solution of being the woman that men are missing".[15]

This highlights very clearly that the informed subject has an access to a compass which orientates his existence. Schreber is informed through his unconscious. It's not the informed desire but rather the informed subject. It gives an indication of the potential treatment for psychosis. Transference helps to seize the marks of the unconscious, whenever the subject has been unable to pick them up spontaneously. The proposition "to be informed by the unconscious" indicates a potentiality, not always possible for all cases. Therefore, I pose that "the open-air unconscious" does not mean that one is necessarily informed by the unconscious. For proof, there exists psychotic subjects who are not at all informed.

The informed subject as well finds its clinical rendering in neurosis. The subject is able to know the situations he has to avoid in his existence.

If we bring forward the analyst's informed desire, how can we make this expression consistent with the question of naivety, because by definition to be informed is to rely on the experience? That is not incompatible, since the informed desire is an informed desire because of the structure. If you know what is the subjects' structure, you know a number of possible impasses linked to the effects of the structure. It does not mean that you know in advance and by experience what is going to happen for such subject. It's rather for the analyst to be informed by the consequences deriving from facts of structure. Furthermore, the analyst is informed by the structure of the analytical mechanism about the conditions that produce a desire. The informed desire is not disconnected from knowledge; it is a desire related to a knowledge about the structure. For example, when one asserts: "in psychosis, we must not interpret", it is a part of the informed desire. One is warned that if you interpret the psychotic subject, it can induce such-and-such effect. At the same time, one notices that to be informed by the structure, one neglects the dimension of singularity. This dimension is an objection to be satisfied with knowledge about the structure. In other words, there exist some cases of psychosis for which the analyst cannot do without the interpretation. There precisely, one notices the limits of the clinic of the subject and by contrast the virtues of the case-based clinic. A case is singular and by definition, does not accept generalizations.

At the same time, what must be understood is that one cannot be completely informed of the effects of speech, for it includes a dimension of incalculability depending on the subject who receives them. As analysis goes on, you take the measure of the subject's singularity, and you know how to handle the speeches which will produce such-and-such effect on the subject.

Hence, the question that we can ask ourselves: do we really know what we are doing as analyst? We know that speech produces effects, it is a fact of analytical experience; henceforth, here it is to be hoped that analytical improvements may occur. Are we always aware of the reasons? Sometimes, it is a surprise for the analysand, but also for the analyst that at this precise moment an improvement occurred, and this because of the effects of these speeches. When the analysand says "what you have told me..." then he develops, it may arise as a surprise for the analyst who does not recognize what he has said, or maybe he has said something else. What is for sure is that the analyst knows what is producing the desire. He knows that an analysis, as it goes on, will produce a change within the subject's relationship to the Other's desire. But he is not certain of the effects of interpretation, nor of the outcome of analysis.

I resume: the treatment orders itself from non-knowledge towards knowledge. So, to know what? To know what one wants to, that is why one undergoes an analysis. So, you know what you want as soon as you mobilize your inner energy. It is to know how to make use of the Name-of-the-Father [*le Nom-du-Père*]. Of course, it is an unconscious knowledge.

To make oneself the dupe of the unconscious

There is another fundamental dimension of the analytical experience which is the de-supposition [*la désupposition*] of the other's knowledge. It must be noticed that Lacan, like Freud, made use of the metaphor of chess games to be able to know the beginnings and the end of the game. For a very long time and mostly by limiting oneself to the reading of "Proposition of 9 October 1967 on the Psychoanalyst of the School", one believed that the beginning of an analysis was the inception of a subject-supposed-to-know, and the end was the de-supposition [*la désupposition*] of knowledge.

It is true that de-supposition [*la désupposition*] of knowledge constitutes an essential dimension in analysis. The experience demonstrates that as we progressively de-suppose [*désuppose*] the knowledge to the Other, we are much more in position to know what we want. Hysteria demonstrates it especially. There exists a tipping point, which happens progressively in the hysteric subject's treatment, which is the de-supposition [*la désupposition*] of the Other woman's knowledge. But there is another dimension of knowledge about the structure, and this is what Lacan, as soon as with his text "The Subversion of the Subject and the Dialectic of Desire", indicates with the "Matheme" S(A). Here, it is not about the clinical structure but rather about the structure of language. In other words, the more a subject confronts the absence of an ultimate signifier which would give the absolute guarantee, the more he is able to accommodate his desire. Hence, desire inscribes itself where the Other's ultimate signifier is missing. Yet, the subject confronts it throughout the treatment, each time he summons the figures which are supposed to incarnate an exhaustive Other. In that sense, the analysis strips the Other, points out his flaws, his inconsistency. For the subject, it results in effects of desire. The emergence of desire is solidary to the analyst's naivety.

When we evoke the analyst's naivety, it is about his position as auditor of the analysand's "spoken words" [*dits*]. It is not that the analyst is naive. He is naive regarding the analysand's statements. Yet, the analyst has a desire and he also has been instructed by his own desire. Lacan formulates it clearly in "Les non-dupes errent", when he reverts to the ethics for psychoanalysis of which he says it "would base itself onto the way to always be more strongly the fool of this unconscious which is ultimately our only lot of knowledge".[16]

He therefore goes further than when he brought forward "an ethics converted to silence", and also demonstrates what he had proposed in his *The Logic of Phantasy*: "The act of keeping quiet does not liberate the subject from language".[17] Indeed, the ethics of analysis is presided by the fact that silence does not exclude speech. From this point is founded the proposition that "The essence of the psychoanalytical theory is a discourse without speech",[18] an axis on which stands the analyst's position.

To be a dupe is another way to speak of naivety; "to be fooled by the structure",[19] Lacan is suggesting in the same lesson. Naivety means to make oneself the dupe of the logic of case. One may say: "there is no case as long as it does not unfold itself in the treatment". The logic of case does not pre-exist. The logic unfolds itself in the improvement of the treatment.

What must also be noticed is the reason why Lacan, evoking the end of the analysis, resumes in the "Proposition of 9 October 1967 on the Psychoanalyst of the School" the question of naivety to indicate that: "thus the end of psychoanalysis harbors naivety".[20]

Why correlate the end of the analysis and the naivety? Lacan refers to naivety in the mechanism of the pass to seize the analyst's desire. Like for the passer, as we said above, Lacan also makes use of the term *naivety*. If he poses it for the passers, it is because the passer "is the pass", that is to say that he places himself at a specific time, just before the emergence of the analyst's desire. Lacan's idea, unlike the institution, the IPA founded by Freud advocates, is that this desire has not to be evaluated by a jury, in the sense that it is not a jury which is at the best place to decide about this desire. That's the reason why Lacan posed that an intermediary must stay between the one who testifies, the passant, and the ones who decide, the jury. Between both is the passer. So, why create complications, create mechanisms, and not demand to So-and-So's analyst, "Has So-and-So truly finished his analysis?", and if he wants to become an analyst, does he have the desire to? Lacan's idea is that the analyst is in no condition to truly answer to that question.

What makes someone at a specific time eager to assume this place? Lacan's idea is that it should be to those who are peers to determine if the passants have established the proof of what they assert, that is to say that the passers have to validate if the passants have been able to demonstrate that they had the desire to become analyst.

So, why put the passer at the core of the pass? Undoubtedly Lacan's idea is that naivety vanishes. It is like everything in life. One is naive at a particular time and as one goes on, one builds walls in regard of what an experience may contain that is more original. It is also for Lacan problematic, and for all who set up as analysts. Are they truly able to remain susceptible to welcoming the surprise of the other's unconscious, or are they installed in a chronicity, with the risk of becoming the official of the analytic discourse? Let's add: if one knows what to do in a particular case, is that enough to attain what makes the singularity of that case?

Besides, when Freud was advocating that to analyze an analyst, it was necessary to renew his analysis every five years, wasn't he proposing a remedy against the analyst who gets so use to his practice that nothing any longer questions him?

It's here that intervenes the logic of case. It's why I pose, that the logic of case is not only the logic of the subject. It takes place between both of them, it is between analysand and analyst. It is between the analysand who is on the path to knowledge and the analyst who has been able to keep up the dimension of the not-known [non-su], up to produce in the cases where the issue occurs, the analysand's desire to become analyst, an original desire.

It is always required to leave an open door to welcome the surprise. And undoubtedly what sustains the analyst in that position is the delight he finds in his practice.

The clinic of detail

We may argue that the case-based clinic is also the clinic of the detail. Sometimes the detail is captured via silly questions, but also it is always through the detail that one sets off towards the exception. In the case-based clinic, what is at stake is to bring out details which clear up the whole. This detail, a gesture, an element of a reminder, an element hidden in a dream, constitutes the best approach to the subject's real. Sometimes, the detail appears only at the end of the analysis, but at times it may be picked up from the beginning and make signs of real. It is not the same real than that of the end, but you must aim to capture it.

I revert to what justifies the evocation of the practice of "chatter", as being susceptible to grab the real. This proposition supposes to pass by translation. Translation consists of seizing the singular language in the subject's statements. It has to do with the question of naivety. It sustains the analyst's following utterance: "You utter these statements, they are known, that's what the current language says, we agree with that, but what do these statements represent for you?". There, we step inside the subject's language, his own language, which differs from all the other ones, the language of his singularity.

It's the meaning of the analysis as a practice of reading, and at the same time we cannot reduce it to that. The analysis also contains the dimension of writing, insofar as the symptom is already a writing inside the body. The question is about knowing what remains out of what is interpreted in analysis. First of all, there is what the subject interprets of his own life's contingencies, but there is also the question of the analytical interpretation. It is an interpretation which introduces a new dimension with regard to the past contingencies, while at the same time preparing those to come. But deciphering the symptom leaves a remainder once the analysis ended. More exactly, an analysis sets in motion in the unconscious a process of writing which continues even when the analysis has ended.

From these considerations, it can be deduced that in analysis you encompass the real only from a position which goes against the semblances. That constitutes the substrate of the analyst's naivety; it is to consider that the whole of what a subject said is no more than semblances. Therefore, naivety is a questioning of the other's semblances. What becomes crucial is to know what is not semblance. Here, Lacan refers to the writing in the unconscious. What in the unconscious is writing itself, which was not written before, and how does the analyst attest it?

Indeed, the writing in the unconscious opposes what is semblance. Semblance by means of myth fills the hole which is in the unconscious, while the writing reduces it. There lies the true efficiency of the analytic discourse. That is to say, that what cannot be said must be encouraged to be knotted differently. With that which cannot be deciphered, because indecipherable or because unutterable, the aim is to see its writing highlighted.

To this end and above all, what's central is how we welcome this dimension of the subject's singular, his own language. Finally, the subject's language is that of his *jouissance*, which resists its absorption by the language and infiltrates into the subject's "spoken words" [*les dits du sujet*], leading to the original symptom. It is why Lacan posed the equivalence between the symptom and the suspension point. It tells us what has still to be written about the symptom. An analysis involves the suspension points, but simultaneously it gives a glimpse to the concluding point. Indeed, what should be considered is the existence of a different point of attachment than the one which was at the origin of the attachment to the symptom, at the time of its inception. Lacan gave a name to the point of attachment linked to the end of analysis, it is the letter, which he defined from the future of the symptom once it has been deciphered. Therefore, it is the letter of the symptom, and it poses at the same time a dimension which persists and does not cease to write itself.

It is why Lacan concluded that the issue at the end of an analysis involves the symptom. Therefrom, one may seize that the expression "to identify oneself to one's symptom" supposes a stopping point linked to what is writing itself in the unconscious. But at the same time, it indicates a motion, an openness, because it begins to write itself, it is not yet written and what is it opened for? It leaves open a door to new contingencies.

The One of exception

It is in that sense that is posed this formulation which Lacan extracts from his text "Lituraterre": "what is elided in cursive script, in which the singular of the hand crushes the universal".[21]

On the basis of Chinese calligraphy, Lacan demonstrates how the painter's brushstroke concerns a singular gesture, proper to the one who makes it, and extracts it from the universal. It is not an act common to the others; here is emphasized that the singular supposes a requirement, to make without the Other and without any model, to tear oneself out of it while giving from our most intimate being. It is a pull-off by which one extracts oneself out of the universal. Without this pull-off, how can we understand Lacan's proposal, concerning the analyst's desire, which links subjectivity and social as soon as 1953? "Let whoever cannot meet at its horizon the subjectivity of his time".[22] Indeed, it is out of the most radical singularity that may result the ability to cope with the most irritating real. Here, we are in the existence and production of the One of exception which Lacan promotes. The One who precedes the analysis, leaves an abeyant subject. The One by the end of analysis is not the same One throughout the analysis the subject believes in. To say that there is the One, is to say that something exists. We often highlight something which does not exist, for instance when using the term of castration or the expression "there is no sexual relationship". Both of these terms indicate what does not exist in the structure and yet determine what exists. At the same time, there is what exists in the structure, and what exists is the One. The One is that dimension of symptom to which he is reduced by deciphering, wherein lies each one's proper identity. That is "the singular of the hand" [le singulier de la main]. That is each one's real, which is the real of the proper difference. That is not the tiny difference mentioned by Freud regarding narcissism, but the true difference, a difference for each one founded by what makes for each one an exception, and which by the end of the analysis will lead to the absolute difference. What must be grabbed is the initial difference, an effect at the starting point of the One's existence, up to producing the letter of the symptom. That justifies Lacan highlighting the virtues of the exception rather than the virtues of the norm.

I resume, extending Lacan's words at the conference of Geneva about symptom. He evokes the case-based clinic, since he states that if we were really handling a case as particular, without placing it into a locker, without referring to experience, our intervention would be different. It is consistent with what I put forward, that our intervention as analyst relies on the perception we are having about what is a case.

I pose that there exists in Lacan the dimension of an advent, the production, the emergence of an unprecedented which he designates as the advent of real. The advent of real, as he says it in "The Third" [La Troisième], does not mean that there was no real before the analysis. There is a real which is already there, and then there is a new real which is the advent of real as affect, out of the analytic discourse.

To pose the case-based clinic as falling in the exception indicates that it does not mean to address the clinic from a question of technical knowledge. Lacan says it differently in The Ethics of Psychoanalysis when he argues: "The analyst too must pay: [...] with what is essential in his most intimate judgement".[23] Judgement implies a statement which does not allow the norm to sustain it, otherwise it would not be a judgement. Judgement supposes that one has quite a few numbers of parameters, coordinates, then one adds another dimension. Therefore, judgement involves a singularity, that is to say that the analyst also utters his judgement. And there exists no protocol to tell him what will be his judgement, it is explicitly stated by Lacan: "an exigency weighs upon the analyst, the one of a judgement".[24] It is also these same terms that he evokes in "The Direction of the Treatment and the Principles of Its Power", the need of a judgement on the analyst's part.

It supposes that the analyst cannot slip away from the dimension of judgement. One may include the passer in this series, when Lacan adds that other dimension to the question of naivety: "the passers dishonor themselves in leaving the thing uncertain, failing which the case falls under the blow of a polite declining of the candidacy".[25] Even in the passer's position, which consists in collecting a testimony, there is a dimension where he cannot slip away: he has to take a stand. When one takes a stand, it is because one assumes a judgement. Therefore, we notice that it's something that we must require at every level of analysis. We must require it from the analysand, the passer, of course from someone being an *AE* [*Analyste de l'Ecole* - Analyst of the School], someone who gave evidences of one's testimony of the analyst's desire and it goes without saying it, we are entitled to require it from the analyst.

It is a dimension which everyone tries to slip away from. Lacan seized its reason even for those who pushed the analysis experience to its final consequences; the analysts. Thus, he formulates "the analyst has a horror of his act".[26]

If we look at it a bit more before the end, we notice that we slip away from the act following specific modalities which are proper to clinical structures. Thus, it's striking for the hysteric subject, and it is the reason why Lacan evokes the "Faithlessness of hysterical intrigue".[27] It is a reference to the expression "faithlessness and lawlessness" [*sans foi ni loi*]. The "faithlessness of the hysteric", that is saying one thing and its opposite without embarrassment in front of the contradiction. It means being the "go-between", those who are mediating, those who refrain to assume her/his own speech. She does not know her own thought or she slips away to say it.

It is often difficult to extract the subject out of a situation consisting in making himself/herself the spokesperson of someone, without really willing to assume his judgement. There is an obsessive slope which corresponds with the "faithlessness of the hysteric", it is the volte-face. In this case it's absolutely striking: the subject asserts clearly his position, then he/she may a moment later, turn over and assert the opposite with the same certainty. Rather than a cop-out, what it is about here is the absence of courage to sustain a judgement.

I resume the subject's knowledge, prior to the analysis. It is a knowledge the subject cannot dispose of; it is the unconscious knowledge. Lacan formulated it in "A record of the analytic act": "To say that there is an unconscious means that there is a knowledge without a subject".[28] Again, it is explicit in the "Geneva Lecture on the Symptom", where Lacan poses: "if there is something called the unconscious, it means that one doesn't have to know what one is doing in order to do it".[29] Then: "Freud observed that there were things of which no one could say that the speaking subject knew them without knowing them".[30] That means that there is what the subject knows without knowing it, and that one does not need to know one knows, for this knowledge is at work.

For a long time, Lacan formulated the unconscious as truth. The unconscious knowledge, it is something else. The entire question is: how to make sure that the subject may have access to this knowledge which is acting unbeknown to him?

When we say the knowledge in the unconscious, we have to single out the knowledge in the real, as Lacan formulates it with respect to science, namely that in science there is also a knowledge which makes things work, whether we know it or not.

Lacan evokes Newton, to whom one asked the question about the planets: "how each mass knew the distance of the others?" and Newton answered: "God, he knows it".[31] It became part of everyday speech, each time one does not know something, one says: "God, he knows it". To say that God knows it, is saying that one cannot know it, but it is at the same time to name the real; "that's known", means: there is a knowledge in real. Knowledge in psychoanalysis, it is something else, since there is a real which is not the real of science, it is a knowledge which is of the order of singularity. This is precisely the analytical knowledge.

In his text "Television", Lacan shows how Kant tries to go against a certain logic when he formulates a critique of reason. Except that he remains in the universal, though he evokes the notion of judgement, as we said above.

It especially interests us, because the case-based clinic is not the clinic of the particular; the clinic of the particular perforce refers to a universal. It is why I insisted on saying that the structure-based clinic is a clinic of particular.

What we want to know in the structured-based clinic is if, from a bundle of symptoms, we may make it converge onto the universal of a structure. There, we have the particular of case and the set which is the structure. That is something else than the logic of case which perforce goes beyond the question of diagnosis and beyond the detection of the structure.

It is what's at stake for us, namely the order to take a position in the experience of the treatment from non-knowledge. Often, there are cases where the question of diagnosis is important, there are cases where the analysis may move forward without having to make a diagnosis. That is to say, that the case does not begin from a diagnosis.

The unique in object *a*

I resume the question of ignorance and knowledge by showing the gap between Lacan and Kant's approach. According to Lacan, ignorance is linked to knowledge, it is not a lack, it is a way to take a stand with respect to knowledge, it is why Lacan spoke of "passion". What is to be expected is that out of this passion, the subject may extract himself to be able to not sustain himself from an established knowledge, because ignorance is an established knowledge: it is to believe that we know.

The established knowledge is the opposite of the learned ignorance it is the sealed knowledge, the knowledge already laid on. What is obvious in the *doxa*, is that ignorance reveals itself insofar as it produces a closure towards knowledge. Psychoanalysis, as a logic of case, is a practice which proceeds against the *doxa*.

According to Kant, knowledge aims to accommodate subject and object. Knowledge concerns what can be observed and represented. In that sense, what is a restriction to knowledge, are the *a priori* conditions of our learning [*connaissance*]. To get used to the objects, therefore to the world, there exists the opinion, the faith, or the knowledge. It is what regulates the relation between knowledge and truth, between subjective and objective. According to Kant, we can consider something as true through three different ways depending on the quality of the reasons which lead you to consider it as true: if the reasons are subjectively and objectively insufficient, we'll talk of opinion [*Meinung*]; if the reasons are subjectively sufficient and objectively insufficient, we'll talk of faith [*Glaube*]; if the reasons are subjectively and objectively sufficient, we'll talk of knowledge [*Wissen*].

Kant limits the knowledge to the learning [*la connaissance*]. And faith appears as a necessary remedy to overcome the limits of knowledge. In any case, Kant emphasizes that in the development of science, it is the initiative of the thinking subject and his *a priori* cognitive structures which found the objectivity. The spirit enforces his *a priori* structures to the world data. Kant points out that it is considering the activity of the learning subject [*le sujet connaissant*], that we may explain the possibility of an objective learning [*connaissance*]. Kant's categorical imperative which states: "Act according to that maxim whereby you can, at the same time, will that it should become a universal law"[32] connects the particular to the universal. Therefore, the knowledge is a means to subjectively represent what is of the order of the object we deal with.

The problem is that to proceed to this accommodation to the object – namely the objects of the world, the objects of the real – Kant poses *a priori* conditions, which are everyone's conditions and determine this relationship with the world. When you pose the *a priori* conditions, you exclude the unconscious. Kant's knowledge is rather in terms of learning [*la connaissance*], that is an understanding of the world, the world of the objects, an understanding from the perception one may have of these objects; one stays at the level of the learning [*la connaissance*]. While knowledge, as Lacan promotes it, concerns a knowledge about the world which is defined by one's relationship with one's unconscious.

When we say that analysis progresses out of non-knowledge, it is because the essence of experience takes its start from "I don't know". The analysand's "I don't know" is accompanied by the analyst's "I don't know", but the latter leaves an open door to a "you may know". That is truly the analyst's position in the experience, and this is precisely and right from the very beginning what the analyst makes the analysand feel.

The analysand's "I don't know" concerns the indeterminacy. It opposes to certainty which is an effect obtained by the end of the analysis. The certainty of the end, what can be expected out of the experience of analysis, is a certainty of knowledge, to know what we want. The question with the analytical experience, is how one goes from indeterminacy to certainty, so from non-knowledge to knowledge.

I resume the case-based clinic from the "object a", cause of desire. When one says, object cause of desire, that means there is something unique in "object a". With the unique, one is in the question of case. What is unique is by definition what makes difference.

The unique in the "object a" is a cause, different from any other one. A cause different from an ideal one. Before the analysis, the subject is driven by desires. The analysis is not the transition from nothingness regarding desire to a yearning subject. Besides, to demand for an analysis, means that initially there is a desire. The question is to know what is presiding over this desire. Most of the time, one notices that it is a common cause. Yet the common cause sometimes is making symptom. In the statements, the subject sustains the cause, but the formations of the unconscious conflict it.

Let's take this example which is far from being unique: a woman whose statements sustain themselves to demonstrate the necessity of gender equality, but whose dreams highlight variants of a similar scene, a woman extremely submitted to a man's sexual desire. Hence her riddle: "Why do my dreams so totally conflict with my thoughts?"

We must not conclude too easily to a desire of submission, but rather to interrogate the interpretation of the unconscious which believes to be able to grasp in this analysand what is the desire for the man. Her unconscious has construed what a man is expecting from a woman, namely to be a submitted woman. In other words, she is split between her unconscious which tells her: the man desires a submitted woman, desire she wants to satisfy and her ideal which makes her feel the requirement of gender equality. What remains pending is to understand the cause of her desire, detached from the collective cause which became symptomatic. If I refer to the ideal, it is because it is an example widely spread of collective causes, the unique cause is something else.

But the unique in the "object a" does not concern only the unique cause. It is also for each subject his elective relationship with the object as "*surplus-jouissance*" [*plus-de-jouir*]. That relationship with "a" as "*surplus-jouissance*" [*plus-de-jouir*] constitutes a modality of *jouissance* that the subject does not share. In this sense, the "object *a*" includes a unique *jouissance* and therefore belongs to the singular.

Notes

1 Lacan, J., « *Le Séminaire, Livre XII, Problèmes cruciaux pour la psychanalyse* », inédit, leçon du 5 mai 1965. ("*Crucial problems for psychoanalysis, Seminar 17*, Wednesday 5 May 1965". My translation.)

2 Lacan, J., « *Le Séminaire, Livre XII, Problèmes cruciaux pour la psychanalyse* », inédit, leçon du 5 mai 1965. ("*Crucial problems for psychoanalysis, Seminar 17*, Wednesday 5 May 1965", p. 256. Translation by C. Gallagher.)

3 Lacan, J., « *Le Séminaire, Livre XII, Problèmes cruciaux pour la psychanalyse* », inédit, leçon du 5 mai 1965. ("*Crucial problems for psychoanalysis, Seminar 17*, Wednesday 5 May 1965", p. 257. Translation by C. Gallagher.)

4 Lacan, J., « *Le Séminaire, Livre XXIV, L'insu que sait de l'une-bévue s'aile à mourre* », inédit, leçon du 14 décembre 1976. (My translation.)

5 Lacan, J., « Introduction au commentaire de Jean Hyppolite sur la « *Verneinung* » de Freud », in *Écrits*, Paris, Le Seuil, 1966, p. 377. ("Introduction to Jean Hyppolite's Commentary on Freud's 'Verneinung' in *Ecrits*", W.W. Norton & Company, New York, London. p. 314. Translation by B. Fink in collaboration with H. Fink and R. Grigg.)

6 Lacan, J., « Fonction et champ de la parole et du langage en psychanalyse », in *Écrits*, Paris, Le Seuil, 1966, p. 259. ("The Function and Field of Speech and Language in Psychoanalysis", in *Écrits*, W.W. Norton and Company, New York and London, p. 215. Translation by B. Fink in collaboration with H. Fink and R. Grigg.)

7 Lacan, J., « Fonction et champ de la parole et du langage en psychanalyse », in *Écrits*, Paris, Le Seuil, 1966, p. 281. ("The Function and Field of Speech and Language in Psychoanalysis", in *Écrits*, W.W. Norton and Company, New York and London, p. 232. Translation by B. Fink in collaboration with H. Fink and R. Grigg.)

8 Lacan, J., « Proposition du 9 octobre 1967 sur le psychanalyste de l'Ecole », in *Autres écrits*, Paris, Le Seuil, 2001, pp. 248–249. ("Proposition of 9 October 1967 on the Psychoanalyst of the School", p. 5. Translation by R. Grigg.)

9 Lacan, J., « Proposition du 9 octobre 1967 sur le psychanalyste de l'Ecole », in *Autres écrits*, Paris, Le Seuil, 2001, p. 249. ("Proposition of 9 October 1967 on the Psychoanalyst of the School", p. 5. Translation by R. Grigg.)

10 Lacan, J., « Proposition du 9 octobre 1967 sur le psychanalyste de l'Ecole », in *Autres écrits*, Paris, Le Seuil, 2001, p. 249. ("Proposition of 9 October 1967 on the Psychoanalyst of the School", p. 6. Translation by R. Grigg.)

11 Lacan, J., « Proposition du 9 octobre 1967 sur le psychanalyste de l'Ecole », in *Autres écrits*, Paris, Le Seuil, 2001, p. 250. ("Proposition of 9 October 1967 on the Psychoanalyst of the School", p. 6. Translation by R. Grigg.)

12 Lacan, J., « Variantes de la cure-type », in *Écrits*, p. 362. ("Variations on the Standard Treatment", in *Écrits*, p. 300. Translation by B. Fink in collaboration with H. Fink and R. Grigg.)

13 Lacan, J., *Le Séminaire, Livre VII, L'éthique de la psychanalyse*, Paris le Seuil, 1986, p. 339.

14 Lacan, J., « D'une question préliminaire à tout traitement possible de la psychose », in *Écrits*, Paris, Le Seuil, 1966, p. 559. ("On a Question Prior to Any Possible Treatment of Psychosis", in *Écrits*, W.W. Norton and Company, New York and London, p. 466. Translation by B. Fink in collaboration with H. Fink and R. Grigg.)

15 Lacan, J., « D'une question préliminaire à tout traitement possible de la psychose », in *Écrits*, Paris, Le Seuil, 1966, p. 566. ("On a Question Prior to Any Possible Treatment of Psychosis", in *Écrits*, W.W. Norton and Company, New York and London, p. 472. Translation by B. Fink in collaboration with H. Fink and R. Grigg.)

16 Lacan, J., « Le Séminaire, Livre XXI, Les non-dupes errent », inédit, leçon du 13 novembre 1973. (My translation.)

17 Lacan, J., « Le Séminaire, Livre XIV, La logique du fantasme », Paris, Le Seuil, 2023, p. 257. ("The Seminar of Jacques Lacan: *The Logic of Phantasy*", p. I.91. Translation by C. Gallagher.)

18 Lacan, J., « Le Séminaire, Livre XVI, *D'un Autre à l'autre* », Paris, Le Seuil, 2006, p. 11. (My translation.)

19 Lacan, J., « Le Séminaire, Livre XVI, *D'un Autre à l'autre* », Paris, Le Seuil, 2006, p. 11. (My translation.)

20 Lacan, J., « Proposition du 9 octobre 1967 sur le psychanalyste de l'Ecole», in *Autres écrits*, Paris, Le Seuil, 2001, p. 255. ("Proposition of 9 October 1967 on the Psychoanalyst of the School", p. 10. Translation by R. Grigg.)

21 Lacan. J., « Liturattere », in *Autres écrits*, Paris, Le Seuil, 2001, p. 16. Translation by the Freudian School of Melbourne.

22 Lacan, J., « Fonction et champ de la parole et du langage en psychanalyse », in *Écrits*, Paris, Le Seuil, 1966, p. 321. ("The Function and Field of Speech and Language in Psychoanalysis", in *Écrits*. W.W. Norton and Company, New York and London. p. 264. Translation by B. Fink in collaboration with H. Fink and R. Grigg.)

23 Lacan, J., « La direction de la cure et les directions de son pouvoir », dans *Écrits*, Paris, Le Seuil, 1993, p. 587.

24 Lacan. J., *Le Séminaire, Livre VII, L'éthique de la psychanalyse*, p. 337. (My translation.)

25 Lacan, J., « Note italienne », in *Autres écrits*, Paris, Le Seuil, 2001, p. 309. ("Italian Note." Translation by S. Schwartz.)

26 Lacan, J. « Lettre au journal *Le Monde* datée du 26 janvier 1980 », ("A letter addressed to the newspaper Le Monde dated 26 January 1980.") My translation.

27 Lacan, J., « Fonction et champ de la parole et du langage en psychanalyse », in *Écrits*, Paris, Le Seuil, 1966, p. 824. ("The Subversion of the Subject and the Dialectic of Desire in the Freudian Unconscious", in *Écrits*, W.W. Norton and Company, New York and London, p. 698. Translation by B. Fink in collaboration with H. Fink and R. Grigg.)

28 Lacan, J., « L'Acte psychanalytique », in *Autres écrits*, Paris, Le Seuil, 2001, p. 376. ("The Psychoanalytic Act", p. 2. Translation by C. Gallagher.)

29 Lacan, J., « Conférence de Genève sur le symptôme », *Le Bloc-Notes de la psychanalyse*, n° 5, p. 6. ("Geneva Lecture on the Symptom", p. 15. Translation by R. Grigg.)

30 Lacan, J., « Conférence de Genève sur le symptôme », *Le Bloc-Notes de la psychanalyse*, n° 5, p. 6. ("Geneva Lecture on the Symptom", p. 16. Translation by R. Grigg.)

31 Lacan, J., « Télévision », in *Autres écrits*, Paris, Le Seuil, 2001, p. 5366. ("Television", W.W. Norton and Company, New York and London. p. 36. Translation by D. Hollier, R. Krauss and A. Michelson.)

32 Kant, E., *Critique de la raison pure*, Paris, PUK, 1968, p. 30. (My translation.)

Chapter 3

From Particular Fantasy

To Singular Symtom

Object *a* as substance

How did Lacan elaborate his conception of "object *a*", which was in his opinion his sole invention in psychoanalysis? It comes in the aftermath of a theoretical reshuffle, this one posing that there is a lack in the Other. Lacan especially performs that process in *Anxiety*. This process lies in the fact that to pose a subject as the effect of the Other's desire, which leaves a remainder, the existence of "object *a*" is on the subject's side. Therefore, "object *a*" is a consequence, linked to the experience of the subjective division and to the absence of signifier on the Other's side. The Other does not have the final say. It is the absence of guarantee coming from the Other. That's what Lacan had developed in "The Subversion of the Subject and the Dialectic of Desire", where he poses that the Other is inconsistent.[1]

He answers that this *jouissance* is forbidden, because "the lack of which makes the Other inconsistent, mine, then?"[2] It is what Lacan connects to this analytical experience, the subject poses the idea of an original fault. It is what religion has captured with the idea of original sin.

Lacan resumes this conception in *From an Other to the other* by giving the status of a substance to "object *a*".[3] Indeed, there must be something on the subject's side substituting for the absence of the Other's guarantee. For a while, Lacan believed that the Name-of-the-Father [*le Nom-du-Père*] could be a substitute for it, which would be the Other of the Other. The Other who substitutes for the Other's lack. It should be noticed that his invention of "object *a*" is attached to the abandonment of this idea. If the Other of the Other does not exist, then what is substituting for the lack in the Other? The answer is the subject's relationship to "object *a*". It should nevertheless be noticed that the subject's relationship to "object *a*", matches the *mathème* of fantasy: ... *a*. Fantasy is a signifying articulation linked to the object of desire. Hence, it identifies a feature. From then, one may seize that the status of fantasy is not for the subject solely linked to his relationship to signifiers, it is also in connection with "object *a*".

As Lacan introduced it from his initial texts, fantasy is a matrix. One may nevertheless find an anticipation of the idea of fantasy as an axiom. Lacan

DOI: 10.4324/9781003568315-4

made use of this term of matrix [*matrice*] in "The Mirror Stage" to point out that it:

> ...manifest in an exemplary situation the symbolic matrix in which the *I* is precipitated in a primordial form, prior to being objectified in the dialectic of identification with the other, and before language restores to it, in the universal, its function of subject.[4]

One may find it as being the conjunction of the imaginary and the symbolic, specific to the function of fantasy as decisive in the formation of a subject's desire.

We also find this term of matrix [*matrice*] in his text "Intervention on the Transference" – again it is coming from a Lacan prior to the outset of his seminar, given that it is in 1951. He resumes Dora's case to emphasize a fundamental scene in her childhood. It is a memory of herself when she was probably still an *infans*, sucking her left thumb, while with her right hand she tugs her brother's ear, this one being her elder by a year and a half. Lacan formulates:

> What we seem to have here is the imaginary matrix in which all the situations orchestrated by Dora during her life came to be cast – a perfect illustration of the theory, yet to appear in Freud's work, of repetition automatisms. We can gauge in it what woman and man signify to her now.[5]

There is no doubt that here, we find the draft of the Lacanian conception of fantasy, and its use, and an articulation which links imaginary and symbolic. If we also consider the automaticity of repetition, we may add that we already find as well the dimension of the real. Certainly, Lacan at first refers to the matrix [*matrice*] in relation to the symbolic, but before having identified the imaginary and symbolic registers. If we read about Dora in "Intervention on the Transference", the sentence about the imaginary matrix [*matrice*] linked to the subsequent Lacan, then it is appropriate to consider the matrix [*matrice*] according to its dual dimension, imaginary and symbolic.

Indeed, according to the terms of the times, the fantasy is a matrix [*matrice*] which assists desire. The subject, throughout his life, but also during his analysis, uses fantasy as a support for desire. Besides, there must be a radical change in an analytical treatment for a subject to take another support than that of this matrix [*matrice*]. But it is already a matrix [*matrice*] which steers the desire towards the *jouissance*, hence what is agreed in fantasy is what guides the subject towards his *jouissance*. In this sense, one may find that the notion of matrix [*matrice*] of fantasy includes a dimension of real, for it steers the subject towards the real of the *jouissance*.

Already, with this approach of fantasy, one observes that desire and *jouissance* do not systematically conflict. It's legitimate to say that fantasy in the speaking being [*l'être parlant*] operates as a substitute for what he misses, for being non-existent in terms of instinct. What is steering an animal towards another one is not fantasy but instinct.

But Lacan takes one more step. A matrix [*matrice*] implies the conjunction of the imaginary and the symbolic, the axiom adds the dimension of a real. Indeed, as soon as Lacan poses fantasy as an axiom, he also poses that fantasy assumes the same place as the real. The fantasy being, at the same time, the index of absence of harmony between both sexes. The subject through fantasy tries to substitute the absence of harmony and to provide the subject with a sexual identity.

As we said, fantasy falls under a particularity. It is what leads Lacan to pose that fantasy, perverse or psychotic, has a neurotic use. Indeed, there are proper uses for each structure. Here, we are in terms of a particularity, a particularity to the use of fantasy, in relation to universal, the one which the uses of fantasy have in common in the same clinical structure. To be able to determine the singularity of a case and to go beyond the particularity, one has to seize the beyond of fantasy, which concerns the relationship between the subject, and his *jouissance*. In other words, "object *a*" compensates for the absence of harmony, but via two ways; through fantasy as we said above, or through *jouissance*.

Lacan formulates it very clearly in *From an Other to the other* where he poses that the big Other [*grand Autre*] is punctured. This idea is correlative to the idea of a lack of signifier in the Other. Hence, he poses that "object *a* is the hole".[6] In this context Lacan introduces the idea of "l'enforme" [*form-taking*], what gives a form a relief, and also what borrows the form.[7] Indeed, Lacan poses that *jouissance* is not unformed. As he says it later in this seminar: "L'Enforme du A [A's "form-taking"]"[8], namely this "*a*" which punctures the Other; "*a*" is the subject himself.

In this seminar, as we already said, fundamental is the conception of "*a*" as a substance.[9] To evoke the substance is something else than to refer to the symbolic. It is suggested on the assumption that Lacan poses, that "jouissance … it is nowhere symbolized, nor is it symbolizable",[10] or when he asserts that sexual *jouissance* is outside the system, absolute. Indeed, to pose it as being outside the system tells us that it is outside the symbolic, and at the same time that it does not let itself become captured or fragmented by it; it remains absolute.

"Object *a*" is precisely what makes a hole, and in the other it occupies the place of the hole. Yet, the key point which emerges in this seminar is that "object *a*" is worthwhile as far as it produces the desire, but simultaneously it concentrates a *surplus-jouissance* [*plus-de-jouir*] on the subject's side.

To the Other's inconsistency responds the subject's logical consistency. Consistency is what responds to the hole. One may say that in Lacan's logic, the subject's consistency falls under what's coming in lieu of the Other's hole. That is fundamental for the analytical treatment, and the more a subject is experiencing the Other's inconsistency, the more he comes close to his own consistency. Consideration should be given to what founds "object *a*". Lacan had already posed its source as being like removing physical samples and had given to the object its modalities: sight, voice, oral, anal. What Lacan introduces in *From an Other to the other*, is "object *a*" as a logical consistency. This is a manner by which to introduce the singular.

Until this moment, Lacan's thesis was that the subject's structure was in correlative relation with the signifier. Lacan poses that formulation: the signifier is what represents the subject for another signifier. This implies the idea that to evoke a subject means at least two signifiers. The signifier as being what's coming through the Other's language, has as a consequence that a subject is the particular modality whereby signifiers fit together.

But I also maintain that the clinic of signifiers is insufficient to approach what is the case-based clinic. The clinic of signifiers is the clinic of subject. The latter says nothing regarding the relationship this subject is having to the *jouissance*.

Once Lacan starts to pose that the body is traversed by the signifier and that it produces simultaneously a mortification, a desert in the body, in the sense of an emptying of *jouissance*, his idea is to pose an area acquiring a special value. Hence, this area focuses on what is removed as *jouissance* from the whole remaining body. The elective localization of *jouissance* on a part of the body provides the indication that this is about *surplus-jouissance* [*plus-de-jouir*].[11]

Therefore, the body figures out his condition in a loss of *jouissance*, it is the body being silent; it is the desert regarding the body. One does not think of the body as long as it is healthy. When there is an illness, one starts to perceive that there exist some parts of the body, one is sensitive to these signs. But there exists an oasis in this desert, a prevalent area where the subject's *jouissance* concentrates dramatically. That is precisely the dimension of "object *a*" as a *surplus-jouissance* [*plus-de-jouir*].

It means that the entry of the signifier into the body produces a decrease on one side, a reversion of *jouissance,* and on the other side a positive conversion. That is why Lacan draws the analogy between his conception of the "object *a*" as *surplus-jouissance* [*plus-de-jouir*] and the Marxian's theory of surplus-value [*plus-value*]. In both cases, there exists on the one hand a dimension of negativity and on the other something in surplus.

Besides, here it is appropriate to emphasize Lacan's criticism against the notion of person. Its etymological root is the mask; therefore, the person is the mask. When one evokes the person, one refers to a dimension which restricts the human being to an identification. There are masks someone is using, but it does not indicate a subjective position. This conception fits with Lacan's distancing towards himself, for he had started by using this term in his doctoral thesis titled "De la psychose paranoïaque dans ses rapports avec la personnalité" [On Paranoid Psychosis in its Relations to the Personality]. Later on, he concluded that he had made a mistake. That is what he asserts in *The Sinthome*: "paranoid psychosis and personality as such do not have any relationship, for the simple reason that they are one and the same thing".[12] That is to say that when one says about someone: "that is a personality", one may have a suspicion of paranoia.

What is a personality? It is a person who is always equal to herself. It is the opposite of a divided subject. When Lacan criticizes the term of *person*, he considers it as being fundamental to comprehend the subject not only in regard of the signifier, but also in regard of the *jouissance* and to extract out of it the clinical consequences. To consider the clinic from the perspective of the signifiers is below Lacan's proposal with the clinic of the *jouissance*. There exists with Lacan a transition from a clinic of the subject to a clinic one could define as a clinic of the *parlêtre* [speaking-being]. Indeed, to evoke the subject in regards to his *jouissance*, he introduces the term of *parlêtre* [speaking-being]. It is precisely where the clinic of the singular locates itself.

There is no other singularity than *parlêtre*

What is the conceptual transition between the subject and the *parlêtre* [speaking-being]? Lacan poses the necessity to refer to the term *I*, as distinct from the term *person*, it is already a first step towards singularity.

He also provides in *From an Other to the other* this definition of the symptom: "the symptom is the way each person suffers in his relationship to jouissance, because he thrusts himself into it via the function of surplus jouissance".[13] With this "each", we are on the side of particularity. But due to the fact that it concerns the relationship with *surplus-jouissance* [*plus-de-jouir*], it provides to each symptom the status of an exception. That is to say, the symptom incarnates what everyone possesses as most singular. The singularity which is not the clinical structure is the singularity of the relationship to *surplus-jouissance* [*plus-de-jouir*].

In this regard, what is interesting is Lacan's definition of the symptom: "the person in other so-called moral registers cannot, from a psychoanalytic perspective, be situated at any other level than that of the symptom".[14] In other words, he proposes to substitute the term of subject of the *jouissance* for the term of *person*.

Lacan attempted to connect the subject and the *jouissance*, but he gave up this perspective. What he maintains is the subject's relationship with his *surplus-jouissance* [*plus-de-jouir*], that is to say his symptom. It is what one finds in "RSI", since he argues that: "the symptom cannot be defined otherwise than by the way in which each one enjoys the unconscious".[15] Starting at *From an Other to the other*, there is thus a progressive abandonment of this term *subject*.

To resume the questions regarding the unconscious and the *jouissance*, there is what's preparing this transitional moment of *From an Other to the other*. That is what Lacan had posed in *The Four Fundamental Concepts of Psychoanalysis*. In this seminar, one finds for Lacan a need to seize another dimension than the symbolic one, since he already addresses the dimension of real. He introduces it with the notion of resistance: he differentiates a resistance stemming out of the ego, from a resistance coming out of an unconscious nucleus. It is a nucleus which is not exclusively linguistic.

In other words, Lacan's idea seeks to draw out the consequences out of what Freud posed as being the repetition compulsion, which is not only the repetition of unconscious signifiers but a beyond to this repetition which is the dimension of a real in the unconscious.

Thus, Lacan makes use of the well-known example: "Father, don't you see that I'm burning", the dream related to Freud, to say that in that dream there is something at stake. Lacan establishes a relationship with the compulsion of repetition where he finds the vindication of what Freuds evokes as neurosis of failure. Something impels failure and it is not exclusively the repetition of the unconscious chain.

It is where Lacan poses this formulation: "the real finds itself, in the subject, to a very great degree the accomplice of the drive".[16] Lacan realizes that one cannot reduce the unconscious to language; it is necessary to seize the unconscious to consider the real.

He asserts it in his critique of the conception of transference which would be only an update of a scene of the past. He reinstates what Freud had left as a toothing stone, namely the authenticity of the love of transference. That is to say, that the transference is not only a repetition with a replacement of characters of childhood by those of the topicality of the subject. Indeed, for Lacan there exists in Freud the draft of what is the real at stake within the transference. Besides, when Lacan poses the "real as the most accomplice of the drive", it is to indicate that in the drive there is something essential: the dimension of failure. Total failure happens each time the drive heads towards an object of satisfaction and fails; it skirts it, it does tricks, but there is always a dimension which escapes, in the sense that the target does not coincide with what was sought.

This question of complicity holds onto the fact that in the same way that there is a failure in the drive, there is a failure in the repetition. In the repetition, there is necessarily something which escapes and that is precisely the sign of the dimension of a real being always at stake.

It is reflected in the clinical phenomena. Indeed, one may notice that when Lacan addresses the clinical structures, it is about a dimension perceived by Freud: the relationship between structures and infantile scenes. That is precisely what Freud starts to pose when he correlates each structure to a scene occurred at a specific date. What Freud is attempting to capture, is the moment when occurred the sexual trauma. At the same time, Lacan extracts the connection with the current *jouissance* singled out by Freud, mainly to clearly set apart hysteria from obsessive neurosis.

Regarding hysteria, Freuds poses a scene which does not generate enough pleasure and for the subject it emphasizes a relationship to the *jouissance* whose trace is the dissatisfaction. This mark for the subject implies a scene without a sufficient satisfaction. It must be correlated with the use of fantasy. Dora sucks her thumb in a relationship to the *jouissance* where nothing would be sufficient. It is the basis of the hysterical daydream, which could be condensed into the phrase "the real *jouissance* is the one which is coming".

Towards the obsessional, as Freud points it out in the Rat Man case, there exists at the start a much too precocious awakening to the sexual infantile curiosity. Unlike the hysteric, it has included too much pleasure, which is a key factor in regard to the *jouissance* within the obsessional. In his case, there is no *jouissance* being up to the one he already met with. That is the source of the nostalgia which defines these cases. Therefore, too little or too much pleasure linked to clinical structures determine subjective positions; the one dreaming about the future, the hysteria, the other turned towards the past, the obsessive neurosis, and none within the present time.

It conditions massive oppositions. That's why I argue that the clinical structures provide benchmarks, these must not be overlooked but remain features linked to a method limiting itself to understand the subject in his relationship to a clinical structure. At the same time, Lacan drafts the distinction between the signifier and the *jouissance*, which is a way to start introducing the clinic of real. What's interesting in *The Four Fundamental Concepts of Psychoanalysis*, with the idea of a decisive scene regarding the relationship to the *jouissance*, is that we are not in the perspective of a maturation, which would be of the order of a progress linked, for the subject, to a libidinal development.

The emphasis is put onto the existence of a contingency, something which intervenes while it has not been planned. Lacan says that it is a "factitious fact"[17]; "factitious" is something which is not necessarily natural. There must be a particularity of the scene; it is what provides the idea of facticity. For example, when Lacan refers to the Wolf Man's primal scene, one finds the scene of facticity. It does not only concern the perception of the sexual intercourse between his parents but a detail of the scene where – as Freud deduces it – the Wolf Man would have seen the in-and-out between the appearance and disappearance of the penis during the intercourse. Therefore, there is a dimension of contingency which in terms of sexuality is the mark of the factitious.

Lacan focuses his attention on the issue of the gaze, and makes use in that respect of the term of split [*schize*], even of profound split, is to indicate something else than the relationship to signifier. For example, let's take the self-reproaches, which refer to the signifying dimension. One reproaches oneself with the help of signifiers. But there is a more profound split, it is the invoking drive. In other words, behind the self-reproaches, there is the relationship to the voice. Here, one may perceive how Lacan introduces another dimension. It is not of the order of the signifier, but instead it is linked to an impulsive object which presides over the subjective position.

Lacan also makes use of the split to criticize Merleau-Ponty's phenomenology as exposed in his book *The Visible and the Invisible* [*Le visible et l'invisible*] which had just been published in 1964. Here, there is the dimension to see and not to see, the visible and the invisible, but Lacan emphasizes another dimension, that of the scopic. What enables the existence of this new dimension? Precisely, it is where comments are fundamental; it's Lacan speaking about the strange contingency linked to lack. The lack is posed in its symbolic dimension as constitutive of the castration anxiety.[18]

This comment is crucial. The question of the case-based clinic is indeed in the line with what Lacan poses as the subject's relationship to lack. I started with the lack of signifier in the Other which makes exist "object *a*" on the subject's side. And precisely here what I evoke is the castration anxiety. That is something else than the lack in regard of the signifying chain. The experience of transference demonstrates it. It is confronting oneself to the lack but first testing it in the Other. From that moment one understands why for Lacan transference is posed in terms of *Che vuoi?* That is to say that where the subject comes across the lack in the Other, he asks himself: what does he want from me?

The answer to this riddle comes from the signifier, but a dimension stays unnoticed and he'll have to test the transference to grasp it; that is his relationship with his enigmatic *jouissance*. It is where truly lies the case-based clinic.

Modality of the "effacings" [*l'effaçons*]

At that precise moment, another fundamental dimension is captured by Lacan; it is the idea of the stain. A stain is what captures us, fascinates us, attracts us. One could elaborate a differential clinic of the stain. A hysterical subject was telling me about the blessedness to be in love and suddenly, to her own surprise, there was a volte-face, unwittingly, with a sharp decline in her love because she suddenly noticed a stain on her lover's face, a stain there since the beginning. She was snatched by the stain while her love was going to pieces. Here, one notices the point of disappearance of the phallus which suddenly adopts a negative connotation. Therefore disappears the belief in the significant phallus being on the partner's side, leading to a sharp decline in love.

In this regard let's go back to this term of effacings [*effaçons*] that Lacan makes use of, at least twice: the first time in "Identification", in his December 1961 6th lesson, then the second time in *From an Other to the other*, in his May 1969 14th lesson. Lacan makes use of the formulation "Effacings of the subject". It is in the sense of the genitive subjunctive and objective for the subject, that is to say that it is at the same time what out of the subject is effacing itself [*ce qui du sujet s'efface*], but also what the subject is effacing [*ce que le sujet efface*]. It is worth reading concomitantly these two lessons, and to cross-reference them. In "Identification", it concerns the signifier, and in *From an Other to the other*, it concerns the drive.

In "Identification", Lacan evokes the effacing [*l'effacement*] of the subject taking the example of the obsessive, and there is a magnificent illustration of lady Macbeth and the bloodstain. Shakespeare wrote that lovely formulation about Lady Macbeth who wants to clean up the bloodstain which does not disappear. Lady Macbeth phrases it like this:

Will all great Neptune's ocean wash this blood

Clean from my hand? No, this my hand will rather

The multitudinous seas incarnadine,

Making the green one red.[19]

The effacing [*l'effacement*] in "Identification" concerns the effacing [*l'effacement*] of the signifying trace: that is precisely what Lady Macbeth can't bring forth. That is the reason why, when Lacan evokes Lady Macbeth, he correlates her with the obsessional neurosis, but not lingering to know if Lady Macbeth was either hysteric or obsessive. That is absolutely of no importance to waste time on. If Lacan gives that example, it is to point out how an obsessional subject may have the use of the signifier, namely to bug the signifier so that it produces a mark. Let me open a parenthesis with the obsessive because it gives an idea about what it is to Lady Macbeth. The obsessive who is affected by the doubt as a fundamental symptom, between two signifiers, spends his time considering either one or the other of the signifiers, being for instance a woman or a professional career. With a line of argumentation and its opposite, he believes he'll be able to produce a consistent object which could give him some certainty in his choice. That is precisely what is problematic about this oscillation between two signifiers: under no circumstances may any of these signifiers rise up to the status of being, for the subject, an ultimate sign. It is precisely what Lady Macbeth is trying to do; she washes, but the stain appears, then she goes on washing again but the stain is still there. It is why Lacan refers to Lady Macbeth because it is precisely the case where the subject is unable to produce an effacing [*un effacement*]. Hence, it is the question of the subject's relationship to the effacing [*l'effacement*] of the signifier. Basically, it demonstrates what is the point of repression [*refoulement*]. Repression is of use to efface, to remove a trace, and therefore not to let it disrupt, and infiltrate the subject's statements. Lady

Macbeth's problem, as for the obsessive, is that while attempting to efface the trace, she effaces herself [*elle s'efface*] as a subject.

Therefore, the effacing [*l'effacement*] discussed in "Identification" is evocative of the operation of repression. It is in facing the event that the subject behaves as if it never occurred. It is the principle of infantile repression. There is Freud's statement – which I consider as superb – about the retroactive cancellation being "a negative magic".[20] It means processing an event as if it never happened.

It is the hocus-pocus performed by the subject who confronted with a fundamental scene out of which must be drawn the consequences, who tells himself: "No, nothing happened". It is the basis of repression, and it's regarding the scene as if it never happened. The becoming subject, thereby, is about the different ways to assume the deleted trace. In *From an Other to the other*, Lacan resumes this elaboration while adding another level, for he singles out the four modalities to efface oneself [*s'effacer*] out of which the subject may take place. These are four modalities in regard of "object *a*". There, these are not clinical structures, but a clinic which is trying to evaluate the subject's relationship with this "object *a*". Out of it, Lacan addresses what it is regarding the Other which left the trace; and what it is about, would be to determine what is making the subject's identity. It's what Lacan will resume in this seminar with his formulation: the "Effacings of the subject".

This question emerges in the seminar, during the May 1969 14th session, when Lacan says: "The subject is who effaces the trace by transforming it into a gaze to be understood here in the sense of slit or glimpse".[21] What is different in regard to the previous seminar is that, then, things were at stake between the subject and the Other, between effacing [*un effacement*] or not, one of the signifiers issued from the Other. But now, it is about the question of emptiness [*béance*], thence the term "glimpse". That is precisely what Lacan introduces as different in *From an Other to the other*, namely that the subject is not only the relationship to the signifiers, but the relationship to different drive-based objects. That's why he speaks about four modalities of "effacings".[22]

Here, it is appropriate to resume what Lacan asserts in *From an Other to the other*, with *l'enforme* [form-taking]. For Lacan, "L'enforme de *a*" [form-taking of a] is a way to refer to the body, namely how the symbolic determines it. In other words, the big Other as being the signifiers' place, becomes this place because signifiers incarnate in a body. And they incarnate in a body insofar as a subject is in connection with his *a*. Thus, the "Effacings of the subject" are the subject's modalities to inhabit the language in his relationship with "object *a*". If one considers the object "gaze", it determines a perspective which is different than the one between the subject and the Other. It assumes the existence of something which does not exactly belong to the subject, neither to the Other, but which is a remainder of the process between the Other and the subject. And for a subject it will condition the modality for adopting a position. In other words, for a subject to exist, one sees the necessity to be effaced [*d'être effacé*]: the subject's effacement is necessary so that "object *a*" may take place, but at the same time the subject, because he adopts a position, effaces it [*l'efface*]. We could correlate it to what Lacan said about Robinson Crusoe, when he evokes the effacement of the trace on a desert island, he chooses the difference between a human being and an animal: an animal may also efface the trace, but what he can't do is pretend, namely to make believe in something else. Here, precisely with this question about effacing [*effacer*] the trace to make believe, we see the dimension of the subject's position.

What's at stake with Lacan's elaboration is the identity. That is precisely what's at stake with the subject's relationship to the drive, what constitutes the identity singling out somebody from somebody else. When Lacan says "the four effacings", in which the subject may take place, that precisely introduces us to the idea that for each one the cut-off produces a process, which is going to delineate a structure of the edge [*structure de bord*] out of which "object *a*" constitutes itself.

With this seminar, we step into a clinic closer to the singularity than the one determined by the clinical structure. That is the clinic of the relationship between the subject and the *surplus-jouissance* [*plus-de-jouir*].

But later on, Lacan, with this phrasing, takes a decisive step when he clearly differentiates symbolic and real: "the real is lawless".[23] It highlights the disjunction between the real and the symbolic. We may go through the symbolic, we may access through the signifiers to the optimal elaboration, nevertheless there will remain a necessary step in order to say: "this is equivalent to the real". That step is impassable. The symbolic is always supposing the existence of a law, the signifying law, while "the real is lawless". Law is a border between these two registers.

There exists on the other hand this definition of the real: "since the impossible is the real".[24] And according to Lacan what defines the real is that nothing is missing. This formulation reflects what Lacan puts forward in regard of anxiety. Anxiety as being an affect of the real is when it "is missing the lack" ["*manque le manque*"]. What is thus specified is something else than a question of intensity, from a progression which would go from disquietude to anxiety. Anxiety fits with a precise conjuncture: the lack has to be missing. That's why the more the analytical experience moves forward, the less anxious the subject is, since the analysis proceeds from the production of lack as a condition of desire. Still, considering that "the real is lawless" and therefore often elusive for the signifiers, the question remains to figure out how a practice of speech can be effective.

The non-function of object *a*

"The non-function of *a*"[25] is a formulation to indicate that "object *a*" is unable to produce the desire. Lacan makes use of it about the mania.

Whether one refers to a specific structure or to a moment a subject is going through, mania sends back to a condition where exists for the subject a dispersion of signifiers, namely a series of signifiers among which there is no lack. That dispersion of signifiers *ad infinitum* operates in a way which is dissociated from "object *a*". That does not mean that there is no "object *a*", but rather that it does not work. The signifiers are not weighted with "object *a*" and the subject stays adrift. Therefore, the function of "object *a*" is to cause desire and to embody itself in the subject's body by giving him a substance in his existence. That's how one notices that in a maniac subject there is a drift, which is not only a language drift, but which expresses itself as his body and his behavior drifting. It's interesting to correlate this notion of non-function of "object *a*" with the notion of the subject's lack of effacement [*d'efface-ment*], since precisely in these cases, the effacement [*l'effacement*] didn't occur. It has to be correlated to a number of psychotic phenomena other than that of mania.

This highlights that each time the subject is in an unprecedented situation, he must mobilize the desire, and he experiences a lack of response. Before a calling which requires the mobilization of signifiers, the subject responds by the absence. It demonstrates that to possess "object *a*" is insufficient, but you also have to be able to make use of it.

This "object *a*" is the residue of the subject's relation to the Other. Lacan will introduce the term of *extimacy* [*extime*], a term which conjoins what is the subject's most intimate with what is his outermost, the most familiar with the most external. It remains external to capture by signifiers because it is out of symbolic.

What's interesting in *From an Other to the other*, and what constitutes a tipping point to Lacan's teaching, is that he is going to provide a definition of "object *a*" not only as being a cause of desire, but "object *a*" "in a position to function as a locus in which jouissance is captured".[26] It means that at the start, there is a *jouissance* that language tends to symbolize. That is a first dimension in the "capture of jouissance" as being the one operated by language. One may see it with children, the more they speak, the less they are agitated, dispersed; they make use of the body to finally make use of the speech.

Yet, one can't equate verbalization and symbolization. Verbalization is an attempt to symbolize. Whether verbalization is sufficient enough to produce a symbolization is dependent on the case. To situate extreme poles, an autistic subject may be perfectly situated in the verbalization – Lacan says that autists are "rather verbose" – and yet he is not in symbolization. To be in the language is a prerequisite, but it is not a condition sufficient enough. It is the same gap between speaking and subjectivation. Let us situate ourselves at a different level, that of sense. We are as close as possible to subjectivation. Sense enables reference to a common thing. With a sense, one may agree upon something by use of the speech, in appearance there exists a pact of speech. One could think that sense is an effect of symbolization. However, it is a fact that one may agree with the other about the sense of something and nevertheless something is missing to attest the symbolization.

When symbolization is missing, the agreement with the other is purely formal. It may as easily be undone as it has been done. Lacan made use of the term *subjectivation* which is the translation to what was, for Freud, the elaboration. The subjectivation indicates an unconscious process as being the indication of signifiers moving to another level than the one of understanding. It means taking a stand in regards to signifiers of one's own history. Then must be considered this other dimension: one may assume the signifiers of one's own history and nevertheless, something from the initial *jouissance* is not resolved; that *jouissance* which is in the body. The body is always traversed by the language which attempts to reduce what makes the advent of *jouissance*: it partially reduces it, but some *jouissance* phenomena persist, variable depending on subjects, and parasitize it.

Lacan poses that "object *a* can function as equivalent to jouissance".[27] One may notice the significance given by Lacan to the term *to function*. The whole issue is: how in an analysis does one make this "object *a*" function in the transference or, as Lacan will argue it later, how in the transference does the analyst proceed to handle "object *a*"? It is precisely in that context where an "object *a*" is posed as helping to capture the *jouissance,* that Lacan provides a new definition to neurosis correlated to "object *a*" and not only to desire. Lacan had delineated the modalities of neurosis as modalities in regards to desire: desire of unsatisfied desire for hysteria, impossible desire for the obsessive, averted desire for the phobic. Yet Lacan, in this seminar, will provide a general formulation for neurosis: "...what is at work with the neurotic's case? Indeed, what is at stake for him is the impossibility of making an object a return to the imaginary level".[28] It means that neurosis is characterized as a maladjustment, a non-accommodation between the cause of desire and the objects of the world. In other words, the subject does not find in the world what may accommodate itself to the cause of his desire. It is the day-to-day experience. It stands as a diplopia of the obsessional. The subject thinks he'll find the woman he has so much dreamed of, then he experiences a diffraction. The object splits itself between the woman of his desire and the beloved one. For the hysteric, it takes the form of a mist, unknowing which object could be convenient to him, or to have it in front of him and be unable to see it. The subjects express it each time they are speaking to us about their disappointments in their friendships, in their sentimental life: the object they come across in the real does not match with the ideal. It does not fit to the cause of my desire. It denotes a flaw between what you come across through life contingencies and what rules the experience for the subject of desire. As we have delineated, what's ruling the subject's relationship to desire is fantasy. In that sense, Lacan poses the equivalence between flaws of logic and flaws of the structure of desire. What does he mean when he talks about flaws? Flaw of logic means that perforce there exists within the logic an undecidable dimension. Gödel demonstrated it with the incompleteness dimension. Flaw within desire ascertains itself in its structuring. For what ordains desire is the grammar of fantasy. This is a grammatical formulation which impels the subject in his existence, giving him an orientation and simultaneously, it turns out that this grammar includes flaws. Lacan's idea is that as for the logic including an undecidable dimension, the grammar of fantasy also includes undecidable dimension.

Therefore, Lacan's idea, when he introduces "object *a*" not only as a cause of desire, but also as *surplus-jouissance* [*plus-de-jouir*], is that there is a locus of the body where the *jouissance* locates itself. The undecidable in fantasy is bound to the riddles of *jouissance*. Lacan asserts it when he poses in *From an Other to the other* that "object *a*" is the place in which to capture *jouissance*. It should be noted that the previous year, in "The Logic of Phantasy", he had formulated a major idea when he had asserted that the Other does not shelter in the mind but rather in the body. Thus, he poses the equivalence between the body and the Other, making of "object *a*" a condenser of jouissance.

It is a major formulation because it poses the idea for what has to be aimed for in a treatment, at the same time for a neurotic subject, but also as far as possible in the process to seek out in psychosis. In psychosis, it means to localize the *jouissance* the subject assigns to the Other. Winnicott was saying it in his own way when he argued that what was to be conveyed to the psychotic subject is that he had not to be scared because things had already happened. Well said. It is another way to state our aim, at least for a few cases of psychosis, that is to say to encase the extensive assignment which, for the psychotic subject, weighs onto the world. What weighs onto him, he assigns to the world, which becomes uninhabitable for it is persecuting him. According to Winnicott, to be able to locate the *jouissance* would be to locate it in the past. If it's in the past, one may box it: it's the past. For sure, it is an intuitive formulation from Winnicott, but it reads differently what Lacan puts forwards with his condenser of *jouissance*. This is about the attempt to determine, to locate, and to fully reduce the surplus exceeding the subject, so that it does not interfere anymore in his life.

Besides, in *From an Other to the other*, Lacan makes use of a phrase which refers to two levels of the graph he produced simultaneously in *Desire and Its Interpretation* and in "The Subversion of the Subject and the Dialectic of Desire in the Freudian Unconscious". In this graph, Lacan marks a lower level corresponding to the imaginary, and an upper level linked to the symbolic, which enables one to situate the drive. Yet, in *From an Other to the other*, Lacan asserts that its function is to produce something at the second level, therefore the symbolic level. It poses the idea that the Lacanian practice does not situate itself at the imaginary level but rather at the symbolic level. Is it sufficient to identify it as a Lacanian practice? In this seminar, there is in addition a definition which poses a new level, when Lacan puts forward that the aim is to produce an effect of symbolic in the real. It is a notion which seems paradoxical to the extent that, as we have explained it, the real is disjoined from the symbolic. Indeed, the question is: How may one touch the real which lacks nothing and is the place of the unconscious where the subject's *jouissance* condenses itself, but which is banned from repression? The effect of symbolism in the real concerns a practice of speech which may affect the *jouissance*. That's the fundamental bet that psychoanalysis is presenting, and which places the Lacanian psychoanalysis as a practice varying from the others, not only from the other speech psychotherapies, but also from the other psychoanalyses.

In that regard, it is appropriate, when Lacan defines neurosis as being a flaw, to resume what he identified as its solution. What's interesting is that we emphasize the neurotic's treatment as a treatment of de-identification. That's true. It is important through de-identification that there emerges a desire which would not be ordered by fantasy. Yet, Lacan's idea – he also formulates it in this seminar – is that the solution to neurosis is not de-identification. If one thinks that it is about de-identifying the subject, why does Lacan consider that it is not enough? He does not challenge the de-identification, but says that it is not the solution.

Hypnosis upside down

There is another step to bring forward, another result to obtain, and it's precisely there that Lacan evokes this formulation which in my opinion is rather enigmatic: it focuses on what happens to the analyst by the end of the experience. Lacan says this: "it is the analyst who is hypnotized".[29] We are only half-surprised. Those who are informed by Lacan's teaching know that in the last lesson of *The Four Fundamental Lessons of Psychoanalysis*, when he develops the question of the gaze, he had already addressed hypnosis as relating to the suggestion. Lacan, again in this seminar, met the challenge of transference where the analysand keeps the analyst in the position of the ideal, a dimension being present throughout the treatment as long as there is a subject-supposed-to-know [*le sujet-supposé-savoir*]. The dimension of a subject- supposed-to-know [*le sujet-supposé-savoir*] possesses as a correlate the dimension of the analyst occupying the place of the ideal. Of course, during the phases – which are not uncommon – of negative therapeutical reaction, which don't lead to a way out of analysis, the analyst is dislodged from the place of the ideal. Apart from these moments, for the subject the analyst often occupies this position of the ideal. In other words, it is by means of idealization for the subject to recover the cause of desire. What is objecting to the analyst remaining in this place is the analyst embodying the position of object, not embodying the position of the ideal. In the terms of *The Four Fundamental Lessons of Psychoanalysis*, it is the analyst who in the transference maneuvers in order to produce a gap between the ideal and the object. In that sense, the analyst goes against what the analysand has relentlessly tried to do, that is to apply a layer of ideal so that he need not confront the cause of his desire. If the neurotic strategy in front of desire is to avoid it, it's because the desire disturbs. Therefore, in that sense Lacan condenses the analyst's position as being an objection to idealization.

As the fiction of the analyst as ideal dissolves itself, the presence of the analyst as "object a" establishes itself more forcefully. The starting position is summarized by Lacan from a mathematical formula: $I(A)/a$. In the numerator, we have $I(A)$, the ideal signifying that which we extract out of the Other and that we pose onto the analyst. Beneath, at the denominator, the formula poses "object a", that is to say what is masked by this idealization. What is covered is precisely the principle of the romantic relationship. In the state of lovingness, what stands at the forefront is the idealization of the beloved object, but the real treasure of love is somewhere else. The idealization overlays the cause of love which at the same time is the cause of desire. There, one sees the analogy between the romantic relationship and the transference.

Nevertheless, love and desire are not homogeneous. One may use love to avoid desire. That is established through the dead-ends of the love of transference. It is a love which shields desire. Thereby, the analyst adjusts his position in regards to the romantic relationship. When Lacan approaches the analyst's status, he evokes this formulation of love which is also the *jouissance*'s one: "*I love you, but, because inexplicably I love in you something more than you, the object a – I mutilate you*".[30] In other words, as well as the lover, the analysand wants to know what is at the core of the incarnated on the side of the analyst. The *"I mutilate you"*, means wanting to see what is the intimate nucleus, the bone constituting the analyst. There, in *The Four Fundamental Concepts of Psychoanalysis*, Lacan poses that the analyst must possess udders, reminiscent of Tiresias.

It is in this context of ending seminar that Lacan provides a definition of hypnosis, namely "to define hypnosis as the confusion, at one point, of the ideal signifier in which the subject is mapped with the a".[31] In the hypnosis, there is a confusion between these two terms, I and a, while the aim of analysis is to maintain the distance between both of them, the ideal signifier, different for each and "object a". Hypnosis is the conjunction of both, that is to say a concentration of both of them at one point. It is the place where the analyst is summoned by the analysand and which embodies simultaneously ideal and "object a". Yet, what Lacan emphasizes is that the analyst's position is what makes an objection, for it aims to produce the gap between both. In other words, the analysis is what keeps the distance between the I of the idealization and "object a", cause of desire.

Lacan has produced a writing of drive, S. D., where D is the demand. The drive is a montage of signifiers which come to the subject out of the Other, for it is the Other's demand which founds the drive. Therefore, to rule out the demand is like trying to rule out the drive. To be able to consider the drive, we must ask: How is analysis proceeding? By allowing the subject to formulate his demands. That is the fundamental reason why complying to the demands does not mean to back up the analysis. When one satisfies the demand, one does not allow the actualization of earlier demands. What's intended, to allow the articulation of the demand, is to leave it open. In this regard Lacan puts forward: "If the transference is that which separates demand from the drive, the analyst's desire is that which brings it back".[32] How is the demand being put aside by the subject? It is ruled out via the identification. The more one identifies oneself, the more one accommodates oneself to the Other's desire, the more one shuts down one's own demand. The risk is the subject making use of transference so as not to be confronted by what his demand may have that is most singular.

Yet, Lacan's idea is that it is not enough for the analyst to ignore the demand. It's precisely why he says that "the analyst's desire is that which brings it back": the desire means reinstating the demand rather than excluding it. In practice, the more the identifications tumble, the more the subject will be able to formulate his authentic demands. Precisely there, Lacan will conclude that the analyst embodies the hypnotized, in an upside-down hypnosis.

Therefore, for the first time in *The Four Fundamental Concepts of Psychoanalysis*, he formulates the analyst as hypnotized. He formulates it again in *From an Other to the other*, but this time, he introduces a nuance. Then he says that the analyst becomes hypnotized, but in a stagnant psychoanalysis: "at least in the form in which it is currently stagnating, it is the analyst who is hypnotized".[33] In other words, it gives the idea that there exists a modification to what Lacan suggests in regards to what he had said with his first use of this formulation: the analyst as the genuinely hypnotized. Is it a contradiction for Lacan? It seems to me that a contradiction is only apparent. If the analyst becomes hypnotized, it's when by the end of the treatment he becomes a pure object which does not cause desire. At the same time, if it occurs in the course of the treatment, with the analyst being hypnotized by the analysand, it does not allow the conclusion of the analysis, and consequently there is a stagnation. It means that Lacan's proposal must not just be a matter of the analyst being hypnotized in the sense of an imaginary fascination for his analysand.

I resume with the drive, which is the writing of the subject's relationship to the demand, and it is what allows us to answer what we've left pending, that is an effect of the symbolic in the real. Thereby, I revisit another session I evoked earlier, that of April 23rd, 1969, in *From an Other to the other*, where Lacan evokes the essence of neurosis. When one says "the essence of neurosis", one could say that it is what allows the assertion of the diagnosis of neurosis. He says that the essence of neurosis is that the neurotic cannot sustain his desire otherwise than through the demand. Therefore, there must be seized how in transference, the subject enunciates his demands. There is a neurotic. Then, what prevents the formulation of these demands?

When one says the demand, it is the subject's demand to the Other, but also the Other's demand about the subject. What is changing in terms of the drive is the index that there has been an effect upon the real. Nonetheless, the subject's real is not only in terms of drive. There is a real which is not captured in the relationship to the drive, since the drive as suggested by the term is the subject's relationship to the demand. Therefore, the drive is in part a relation to the signifier and in part a relation to the *jouissance*. There occurs the articulation between the symbolic and the real. In other words, may this real of *jouissance* be affected?

I resume the question of hypnosis. Lacan, in *The Four Fundamental Concepts of Psychoanalysis*, takes Freud's text, *Group Psychology and the Analysis of the Ego*, as a fulcrum. In chapter VIII of this book, "The feeling of love and hypnosis", Freud differentiates the genuine love from the question of sexual desire, in other words love beyond the pure sexual enjoyment. Indeed, that processing raises a question which is: why does one choose a partner rather than another one, and why does one maintain it lastingly or at least for a while? That is Freud's question: once one has gotten sexual satisfaction, what makes one remain with the partner? Once again Freud summons the term of *idealization* which consists of processing the object as the subject's proper ego. That is to say that one loves in the other what one would like to be, without being able to. There Freud evokes love as narcissistic: the object taking the place of the ego's ideal. Therefore, Freud poses, as we showed, the similitude between hypnosis and the feeling of love. Lacan, on this point, will keep up with him by addressing hypnosis as a two-person entity, that is to say that it operates with two in the same way as in a crowd. It is sufficient to find in a crowd a place for the ideal, the one held by the leader, to seize the relationship model of the hypnotized to the hypnotist. The fascination exercised onto the other is the common factor between the hypnotist and the leader of a mob. It can go as far as adopting a mystical character. Lacan makes use of this detection to display how the ego's ideal operates from what he writes as i(a), that is to say the image of the narcissistic object. Therefore, he extends Freud's proposal to demonstrate that there exists a difficult item to seize in hypnosis, which is the object gaze. Therefore, one goes back to the stain mentioned previously. The perception of the stain is posed by Lacan as being prior to the sight, that is to say one is enthralled by the stain. The stain attracts us. Therefore, it is from the process of producing the gap between the capital I of the idealization and "object *a*", cause of desire, that one may aim at the subject's point of lack, what causes it, "object *a*"; it is precisely there that Lacan evokes the analyst in a kind of upside-down hypnosis where the analyst embodies the hypnotized. It must be said that it is a strange formulation.

What is a hypnotized person? One could agree in saying that a hypnotized person is someone who is not a subject. That is someone who is in a position of fascination in regard to the other. If one argues that hypnosis is like the mob, it means that, as in the mob, there is no subject; everyone is submitted to the signifier of the ideal which drives it. In hypnosis, it is the same, the hypnotized is someone who is dismissed as a subject. When Lacan says "upside-down hypnosis", I tend to think that what is taking place in this "upside-down" is that, for a while, the analyst who has embodied the *agalmatic* [*agalmatique*] "object *a*" for the analysand, becomes the hypnotized in the "object *a*" section by the analysand's side. That does not mean that to end the analysis, the analyst has to be fascinated by the analysand!

What Lacan is asserting is his later draft proposal, is the analyst as refuse. It is Lacan's thesis that, by the end of the treatment, the analyst turns into refuse, rubbish, even "determined refuse". If the end of the process means that there is no more subject-supposed-to-know [*le sujet-supposé-savoir*] but a hypnotized object, then logically one may let it fall. The formulation "the hypnotized analyst" leads to confusion but also prepares the analysand for what is becoming of the analyst. Lacan makes use of the expression of *"désêtre"* [dis-being]. The *désêtre* is not a lack-of-being, but rather the non-being. This non-being has to do with reducing the Other to a pure hypnotized object. To this end, there exist a means, it is what Lacan names "This crossing of the plane of identification".[34] It is precisely where there exists a clear-cut partition between the Lacanian psychoanalysis and the IPA's psychoanalysis. Lacan suggests at the end of *The Four Fundamental Concepts of Psychoanalysis* an exploration of how the subject is living the drive once the experience of the fundamental fantasy has been traversed. For Lacan, the question is no longer about what is remaining of the identifications, since one assumes that the identifications – including the analyst's one – must plummet, but is about the subject's relationship to the drive. That is precisely what relates to the analyst's desire, since Lacan at the time is already posing that the analyst's desire must be correlated to the way the subject is living the drive after having traversed the fantasy.

Notes

1 Lacan, J., « Subversion du sujet et dialectique du désir dans l'inconscient freudien », in *Écrits*, p. 820. ("The Subversion of the Subject and the Dialectic of Desire", in *Écrits*, W.W. Norton and Company, New York and London, pp. 694–695. Translation by B. Fink in collaboration with H. Fink and R. Grigg.)
2 Lacan, J., « Subversion du sujet et dialectique du désir dans l'inconscient freudien », in *Écrits*, p. 820. ("The Subversion of the Subject and the Dialectic of Desire", in *Écrits*, W.W. Norton and Company, New York and London, pp. 694–695. Translation by B. Fink in collaboration with H. Fink and R. Grigg.)
3 Lacan, J., *Le Séminaire, Livre XVI, d'Un Autre à l'autre*, p. 45. (*From an Other to the other: The Seminar of Jacques Lacan, Book XVI*, p. 46. Translation by B. Fink.)
4 Lacan, J., « Le stade du miroir comme formateur de la fonction du Je », in *Écrits*, Paris, Le Seuil, 1966, p. 94. ("The Mirror Stage as Formative of the *I* Function", in *Écrits*, W.W. Norton and Company, New York and London, p. 94. Translation by B. Fink in collaboration with H. Fink and R. Grigg.)

5   Lacan, J., « Intervention sur le transfert », in *Écrits*, Paris, Le Seuil, 1966, p. 221. ("Presentation on Transference", in *Écrits*, W.W. Norton and Company, New York and London, p. 180. Translation by B. Fink in collaboration with H. Fink and R. Grigg.)

6   Lacan, J., *Le Séminaire, Livre XVI, d'Un Autre à l'autre*, p. 45. (*From an Other to the other: The Seminar of Jacques Lacan, Book XVI*, p. 45. Translation by B. Fink.)

7   Lacan, J., *Le Séminaire, Livre XVI, d'Un Autre à l'autre*, p. 45. (*From an Other to the other: The Seminar of Jacques Lacan, Book XVI*, p. 46. Translation by B. Fink.)

8   Lacan, J., *Le Séminaire, Livre XVI, d'Un Autre à l'autre*, p. 311. *From an Other to the other: The Seminar of Jacques Lacan, Book XVI*, p. 312. Translation by B. Fink.)

9   Lacan, J., *Le Séminaire, Livre XVI, d'Un Autre à l'autre*, p. 315. *From an Other to the other: The Seminar of Jacques Lacan, Book XVI*, p. 312. Translation by B. Fink.)

10 Lacan, J., *Le Séminaire, Livre XVI, d'Un Autre à l'autre*, p. 321. *From an Other to the other: The Seminar of Jacques Lacan, Book XVI*, p. 278. Translation by B. Fink.)

11 Lacan, J., « Radiophonie », in *Autres écrits*, p. 409. ("Radiophonie", pp. 4–5. Translation by J.W. Stone.)

12 Lacan, J., *Le Séminaire, Livre XXIII, Le sinthome*, p. 53. (*The Sinthome: The Seminar of Jacques Lacan, Book XXIII*, p. 41, Polity Press, Cambridge, 2016. Translation by A.R. Price.)

13 Lacan, J., *Le Séminaire, Livre XVI, d'Un Autre à l'autre*, p. 41. (*From an Other to the other: The Seminar of Jacques Lacan, Book XVI*, p. 29. Translation by B. Fink.)

14 Lacan, J., *Le Séminaire, Livre XVI, d'Un Autre à l'autre*, pp. 317–318. (*From an Other to the other: The Seminar of Jacques Lacan, Book XVI*, p. 275. Translation by B. Fink.)

15 Lacan, J., *Le Séminaire, Livre XXII, RSI*, Leçon du 18 février 1975. (*The Seminar of Jacques Lacan, Book XXII*, p. 111. Translation by C. Gallagher.)

16 Lacan, J., *Le Séminaire, Livre XI, Les quatre concepts fondamentaux de la psychanalyse*, Paris, Le Seuil, 1973, p. 67. (*The Four Fundamental Concepts of Psychoanalysis Seminar of Jacques Lacan, Book XI*, p. 69. Translation by A. Sheridan.)

17 Lacan, J., *Le Séminaire, Livre XI, Les quatre concepts fondamentaux de la psychanalyse*, Paris, Le Seuil, 1973, p. 67. (*The Four Fundamental Concepts of Psychoanalysis Seminar of Jacques Lacan, Book XI*, p. 70. Translation by A. Sheridan.)

18 Lacan, J., *Le Séminaire, Livre XI, Les quatre concepts fondamentaux de la psychanalyse*, Paris, Le Seuil, 1973, p. 69. (*The Four Fundamental Concepts of Psychoanalysis Seminar of Jacques Lacan, Book XI*, p. 72. Translation by A. Sheridan.)

19 Shakespeare, W., *Macbeth*, Act 2, Scene 2, p. 1059. *The Complete Works of William Shakespeare*. The Alexander Text introduced by Peter Ackroyd. London, HarperCollins, 2006.

20 Freud, S., *Inhibitions, Symptoms and Anxiety, The Standard Edition*, W.W. Norton and Company, September 17th 1990.

21 Lacan, J., *Le Séminaire, Livre XVI, d'Un Autre à l'autre*, p. 314. (*From an Other to the other: The Seminar of Jacques Lacan, Book XVI*, p. 271. Translation by B. Fink.)

22 Lacan, J., *Le Séminaire, Livre XVI, d'Un Autre à l'autre*, pp. 314–317. *From an Other to the other: The Seminar of Jacques Lacan, Book XVI*, pp. 271–275. Translation by B. Fink.)

23 Lacan, J., *Le Séminaire, Livre XXIII, Le sinthôme*, p. 137. (*The Sinthome: The Seminar of Jacques Lacan, Book XXIII*, p. 41. Polity Press, Cambridge, 2016. Translation by A.R. Price.)

24 Lacan, J., *Le Séminaire, Livre XIV, La logique du fantasme*, Leçon du 10 mai 1967. (*The Logic of Phantasy: The Seminar of Jacques Lacan, Book XIV*, p. 129. Translation by C. Gallagher.)

25 Lacan, J., *Le Séminaire, Livre X, L'angoisse,* Paris, Le Seuil, 2004, p. 388. (*Anxiety: The Seminar of Jacques Lacan, Book X*, p. 312. Translation by C. Gallagher.)
26 Lacan, J., *Le Séminaire, Livre XVI, d'Un Autre à l'autre,* p. 249. *From an Other to the other: The Seminar of Jacques Lacan, Book XVI*, p. 214. Translation by B. Fink.)
27 Lacan, J., *Le Séminaire, Livre XVI, d'Un Autre à l'autre,* p. 249. (*From an Other to the other: The Seminar of Jacques Lacan, Book XVI*, p. 213. Translation by B. Fink.)
28 Lacan, J., *Le Séminaire, Livre XVI, d'Un Autre à l'autre,* p. 261. (*From an Other to the other: The Seminar of Jacques Lacan, Book XVI*, p. 255. Translation by B. Fink.)
29 Lacan, J., *Le Séminaire, Livre XVI, d'Un Autre à l'autre,* p. 278. (*From an Other to the other: The Seminar of Jacques Lacan, Book XVI*, p. 241. Translation by B. Fink.)
30 Lacan, J., *Le Séminaire, Livre XI, Les quatre concepts fondamentaux de la psychanalyse,* Paris, Le Seuil, 1973, p. 241. (*The Four Fundamental Concepts of Psychoanalysis: The Seminar of Jacques Lacan, Book XI*, p. 268. Translation by A. Sheridan.) Emphasis in original.
31 Lacan, J., *Le Séminaire, Livre XI, Les quatre concepts fondamentaux de la psychanalyse,* Paris, Le Seuil, 1973, p. 241. (*The Four Fundamental Concepts of Psychoanalysis: The Seminar of Jacques Lacan, Book XI*, p. 273. Translation by A. Sheridan.)
32 Lacan, J., *Le Séminaire, Livre XI, Les quatre concepts fondamentaux de la psychanalyse,* Paris, Le Seuil, 1973, p. 241. (*The Four Fundamental Concepts of Psychoanalysis: The Seminar of Jacques Lacan, Book XI*, p. 273. Translation by A. Sheridan.)
33 Lacan, J., *Le Séminaire, Livre XVI, d'Un Autre à l'autre,* p. 278. (*From an Other to the other: The Seminar of Jacques Lacan, Book XVI*, p. 241. Translation by B. Fink.)
34 Lacan, J., *Le Séminaire, Livre XI, Les quatre concepts fondamentaux de la psychanalyse,* Paris, Le Seuil, 1973, p. 245. (*The Four Fundamental Concepts of Psychoanalysis: The Seminar of Jacques Lacan, Book XI*, p. 273. Translation by A. Sheridan.)

Chapter 4

The Case-Based Clinic in Psychosis

Choice of structure

I resume what Freud formulated as "the choice of neurosis", which may articulate itself out of what Lacan had introduced as "the unsoundable decision of being".[1] I resume here a formulation read out of *From an Other to the other*. It gives an indication about causality but also about handling transference. Lacan asserts: "Its sole mainspring is always, of course, found in the way in which the father's and mother's desires presented themselves – in other words, the way in which they in fact offered knowledge, *jouissance*, and object *a*".[2] Thus, Lacan refers to causality and to what for him seems fundamental, the offer proposed to the subject: knowledge, *jouissance*, and "object *a*". The quotation continues: "this is what must consequently incite us to not merely explore the subject's history". That is a fundamental comment for the clinic: what is central is that it does not mean to practice anamnesis, nor give a narrative of how things historically took place.

The quotation goes on to say: "but the way in which each of these terms was offered to him". It's accurate. What is crucial is the relationship father and mother have had to knowledge, to *jouissance*, and to cause of desire. Lacan's quotation continues: "therein lies what we improperly call 'the choice of neurosis' or even the choice between psychosis and neurosis". Therefore, here he draws attention to a fact linked to his time but which is still relevant. It is about questioning the causality, since he refers to "what we improperly call the 'choice of neurosis'". Here, it is Lacan who retraces his steps and puts forward a strong thesis:

> There was no choice, for the choice was already made at the level of what was presented to the subject, but that can only be located and perceived as a function of the three terms I have just tried to bring out for you.[3]

This proposal is about a clarification of the causality, particularly what we may understand as the choice of structure.

DOI: 10.4324/9781003568315-5

Usually, one understands the formulation "the unsoundable decision of being" as the idea that there exists, regarding the structure, a subject's unconscious choice. Yet, here Lacan's claim is that for the subject there is no other option than the possibility to cope with what has been offered to him. And what has been offered, one can't change. For him, it is registered in the facts. These are the contingencies which have been submitted to him. To deal with them is up to him. But for each parent, the relationship he has with knowledge, *jouissance*, and "object *a*" – being the cause of desire – is something immutable. Nevertheless, with this new proposition from Lacan, there is what stays unchanged in regard to what he had argued previously, in particular in "On a Question Preliminary to any Possible Treatment of Psychosis". Indeed, in this text Lacan poses as essential in the causality of the child's structure, the place a mother reserves to the father's speech, but the opposite as well. In *From an Other to the other*, what's becoming central is the relationship the parents sustained in terms of desire and *jouissance*. What is certain is that with this new proposition about "the choice of neurosis" in *From an Other to the other*, the degree of choice regarding the structure is greatly reduced. Is it therefore "the unsoundable decision of being" being put into question? I don't think so. It is a clinical fact. Moreover, according to Lacan's terms, one could deduce that the parents who effectively offered to the subject knowledge, *jouissance*, and "object *a*", created the conditions that may produce a case of psychosis: nevertheless, the result does not establish it. That is the best evidence that there is no possibility of framing a predictive clinic or anticipation of risks. Indeed, the clinic is filled with surprises, and subjects facing the few things which have been offered to them, demonstrate for themselves an ability to invent favorable solutions. The opposite is true too, and alleged favorable conditions do not deliver the expected result.

In this sense, I resume a classic argument in the Lacanian psychoanalysis. There is a fairly widespread doxa which seeks to oppose neurosis and psychosis about desire and subject-supposed-to-know [*le sujet-supposé-savoir*]: neurosis would be the desire and the establishment of the subject-supposed-to-know [*le sujet-supposé-savoir*], and in contrast psychosis would be banned from any relationship to desire and subject-supposed-to-know [*le sujet-supposé-savoir*]. Yet very early on, Freud poses that what is crucial is the dimension of transference. Somehow, by formulating it, he put in perspective the question of diagnostic. What seems essential for him, is the subject's ability to develop a transference. In psychosis, it is problematic to suppose any knowledge on the Other's side; the subject establishes himself as someone who's knowing and therefore in a position which falls under: "there is nothing to know" or "it is impossible to accede to any knowledge". That is the principle of erotomania: the erotomania, as conviction to be loved, but as well as love addressed to the other with a confidence of reciprocity, does not imply it is a love which is conditioned by the fact to address itself to knowledge. It does not exclude from transference the psychotic subject. It is rather the erotomania in psychosis which is the basis of transference. It's required to resume Lacan's formulation: "in the beginning of psychoanalysis is the transference".[4] It's for Lacan a way to resume a psychoanalytic fundamental axis, already anticipated with the formulation marking the beginning of the seminar *The Transference*: "at the beginning of analytic experience [...] was love".[5]

This "in the beginning" has to be understood rigorously, because sometimes to begin an analysis one takes the preliminary interviews only as a phase to identify the diagnostic, while what it is about with "in the beginning of psychoanalysis is the transference", is that at the outset it implies the analysand commitment in the experience. According to Freud, it is not just about evaluating transference but also stirring it up. A transference which does not speak to the subject-supposed-to-know [*le sujet-supposé-savoir*] does not mean to exclude the psychotic from the analytical system. Therefrom, once the analysis is active for the psychotic subject, the question is about desire. There are quite a few of Lacan's remarks which tell us that he does not pose a disjunction between desire and psychosis. Thus, in *Psychosis*: "the distinction I drew last time between the realization of repressed desire on the symbolic level in neurosis and on the imaginary level in psychosis".[6] Therefore, this former formulation does not exclude the desire for the psychotic subject, but rather opposes the desire: on the symbolic side in neurosis, on the imaginary side in psychosis. Then he adds, in reference to psychosis: "delusions are indeed legible, but they are also transcribed into another register".[7] Therefore, delusion is discussed as an imaginary formation, in the same way Lacan poses fantasy as cause of desire. Delusion as an imaginary formation for Lacan is a way to pose what Freud designated as an attempt of healing. Therefore, there is a desire at work in the attempt of healing, the signifiers do not order themselves at random, it is the subject who handles them in the quest for a resolution. Freud had written to Fliess: "Thus these people love their delusion *as they love themselves*".[8]

Admittedly, it is valid for the delusion as an attempt to explain the subject, but it is less obvious during the outset phases, when the subject revolts himself against what he feels as intrusive ideas. This is resumed in *The Formations of the Unconscious*:

As psychotic I try to establish in the other this desire which is very precisely this function, this essential relationship which is not given because I am psychotic, because nowhere has there been produced this essential metaphor which gives to the desire of the Other this primordial signifier, this signifier which is called the signifier phallus.[9]

Therefore, here is the idea that there exists a missing dimension in psychosis, but also its counterpart, an attempt to what Lacan calls "to institute something in the Other" which requires, as posed by Lacan, a psychotic subject's desire. We also have to perceive the proximity between "to institute in the Other", according to Lacan's terms, and the attempt of healing.

In the same direction, in "On a Question Preliminary to any Possible Treatment of Psychosis", Lacan does not hesitate to designate – resuming Freud's term – the asymptomatic character in Schreber's delusion, indicating the asymptomatic realization of desire. In other words, with Schreber there exists in the resolution of the impasse produced by the emergence of signifier in the real, an asymptomatic solution which came to him via his desire. It explains how delusion has a dimension of healing, but also that there is something which pushes towards a subject's desire. Therefore, the legible desire in the delusion gives us the idea of a potential identification in psychosis, and even an identification to what is functioning as phallus, even if it is not the symbolic dimension.

We have demonstrated it about Schreber since the solution came to him because he has been informed by the unconscious. This highlights that the question is not only posed between deciphering the unconscious in neurosis and no deciphering at all in psychosis. When one poses that the subject is informed by the unconscious, it gives us the idea that the analyst's position is not only to be a witness of the psychotic. It's true to say that the analyst stands as the listener of the psychotic subject's testimony which, since Lacan, leads to the famous formulation: "the secretary of the insane". Admittedly the analyst stands as a witness, but I consider that this side of "informed by the unconscious" introduces another dimension. It gives us a completely different clinical perspective of psychosis under transference. How may we lead the subject to be better informed via transference, to what must guide him in his existence? It's a fact that there exists a knowledge the subject can read out under transference. Therefore it tones down the non-supposition of knowledge in psychosis, yet does not reduce the treatment in psychosis to the fact of becoming "the secretary of the insane".

We must keep in mind what Lacan says regarding Joyce, the one for whom he also makes use of the term *desire*:

> Isn't his desire to be an artist who would keep the whole world busy, or in any case as many people as possible, what compensates exactly for the fact that, let's say, his father was never a father for him?[10]

That someone was able through writing to reduce the symbolic to the real – that is precisely Lacan's demonstration – does not mean that he is excluded from desire, because at the same time what is driving him is a desire of recognition. The symbolic becomes real, but on the horizon, there is that desire which is not of a pure *jouissance* of the letter. Obviously, neither Schreber nor Joyce have ever been in analysis, but they are supporting the possibility to consider how under transference there may be a reshuffle of case, to the extent that the subject supports himself from what would be his own desire extracted out of transference.

What's striking is what Lacan is calling "pure desire, the pure and simple desire of death as such"[11] in Antigone, in *The Ethics of Psychoanalysis*, and what must be connected with a formulation which constitutes the core of this seminar: "Have you acted in conformity with the desire that inhabits you?"[12] It requires a remark: this formulation has to be correlated with the desire in psychosis, since Lacan refers to a pure desire. I affirm that each time Lacan is making use of a "pure" signifier, one must be suspicious and ask himself if he does not refer to psychosis. For Antigone, after the pure desire, he adds: "desire of death". It is weird because a desire, in theory, is a desire which is on the side of life, therefore desire of death is a formulation which is there to indicate a decided character of the subject's decision which drives him towards death. For me, it seems incompatible to affirm at the same time desire and death, the existence of a desire which pushes toward death. The fact that Lacan adds: "desire dramatically destructive", further confirms this hypothesis.

In *The Ethics of Psychoanalysis*, Lacan argues about Antigone's mother that "the desire of the mother[…] is seminal to the whole of the structure". He utters these words ten years before what he evokes as the "choice of neurosis" in *From an Other to the other*. Thus, I wonder if Lacan was not already having the idea that the subject's structure is there, because of this desire of the mother. Lacan does not dither: Antigone made a choice facing the way her brother's non-funeral took place. Her choice is precisely there, it is a decided desire, but the structure, Lacan poses, had already been decided before, through Antigone's mother's deadly desire. He even poses the existence of a criminal desire from Antigone's mother. And it is in this sense that he asserts that Antigone incarnates the pure desire. Incarnates pure desire, but the desire in its purest destructive way, without any division by the symbolic and which was already there, through the way it was founded by the mother. Then he adds even more when he establishes the link between Antigone and Hamlet, since he poses that for Hamlet the same thing occurred. It also indicates for Hamlet the existence of a familial constellation which leaves the subject with very few choices. Something happened between the parents, at the level of desire and *jouissance*, leaving the subject in an impasse. This leads Lacan to say that Antigone's impasse is similar to Hamlet's. That being said, Lacan adds, crucially, "but more dramatic", obviously in reference to Antigone. This is confirmed when he refers to Antigone with these terms: "There is no one to assume the crime and the validity of crime apart from Antigone".[13] Ultimately, Antigone's choice was a choice of assumption; she assumes this criminal desire of the mother and what Lacan calls the validity, that is to say that she goes all the way. This is her choice. It'd be appropriate to connect Antigone's pure desire with the analyst's desire, which is not, as Lacan asserts it in *The Four Fundamental Concepts of*

Psychoanalysis, a pure desire. Indeed, it makes it possible to measure what they have in common and what separates them. There exists in the analyst's desire a dimension of intransigence, determined to go all the way, without any compromise. It is a desire which aims the absolute difference. Yet, highlighting that it is not a pure desire, it tells us its links to the symbolic, to the law, to dialectics. The not-pure [*le pas-pur*] of the analyst's desire tells us that it is not a desire heading towards death. Lacan was formulating it otherwise but in the same direction, the analyst's desire cannot be a desire of the impossible. It is a desire standing on the side of life.

The choice in psychosis

In Lacan there is a formulation about neurosis, but one may wonder how it may be relevant to psychosis. It's when Lacan indicates that the end of an analysis is "to identify to one's symptom". Obviously, often one asks the question: if a psychotic subject meets with an analyst, how may it end? When Lacan says "to identify to one's own symptom", he adds "to identify oneself while taking some insurance, a kind of distance".[14] This formulation, which concerns the future of symptom in analysis, could also enlighten us about what for a psychotic subject could in a psychoanalysis be waited for, expected, that he may gain "a kind of distance". A distance is something else than negation of the existence or non-liability. The idea of taking some distance supposes that the subject has assumed his part of responsibility in his symptom. In analysis, it is the subject's problematics who entrusts to the Other the task of the cause, the supposition of knowledge. To pose the object causing the desire on the Other's side is not to assume the task; therefore there is, throughout an analysis, a subject shifting the responsibility onto the analyst. It is the principle of supposition. The supposition is a supposition of existence. To suppose, it's believing there is something even if there is nothing. The problem is that for the psychotic subject it is not a supposition. The object, he has it, he does not suppose it, it's on his side, so there is nothing to suppose. It is the reason Lacan said, regarding the psychotic subject, that "he does not care about the Other, the big Other, via the object *a*, the *a* is at his disposal".[15]

Regardless, a number of psychotic's subjects meet with an analyst and then continue the treatment. There, the question of distance takes place. It also involves a clinical question in psychosis, particularly regarding the Thing [*la Chose*]. Lacan also penned the Thing [*la Chose*] as "*l'Achose*". When Lacan says "*L'Achose*", there is a pun between two terms *la* and *chose*; and when Lacan writes "*l'A*", it means that in lieu of *la Chose* [the Thing], that is to say what for someone is the most valuable, in lieu of setting it on the Other's side, in psychosis the subject sets it on his side. To write "*A-majuscule-chose*" [A-capital-letter-thing], in the same word, is a lovely manner of saying that there is something within oneself, but which operates as the Other of oneself.

Therefore this "*L'Achose*" inside oneself is characterized by the fact that it is not an imaginary figure. One cannot imagine this Other inside oneself, and besides it, it is a non-representable [*insymbolisable*] remain. Therefore, with a psychotic subject, often the clinic works to create a wall regarding this Thing [*cette Chose*]. To create a wall is a way to keep some distance. That is what I have formulated by: to encapsulate the *jouissance*. It protects against this Thing [*cette Chose*] which is a real of *jouissance*, which tirelessly and identically comes back and which one cannot consider as a repetition, because a repetition by design wears out. After a while, with repetition there is a depletion. In psychosis, with the return there is no depletion, it's a return to the identical. With Lacan, it is what one may designate as a return to the *jouissance* in psychosis, that is to say a return to the real or, according to the formulation "On a Question Prior to Any Possible Treatment of Psychosis", it would be a return of "signifier to the real". This suggests that speech prevails for the subject, but it could be an affect. Recently, a subject was telling me: "But how is it that, without any reason, I suddenly feel gloomy and that after this, for two or three days I am in a bad mood and without understanding why, without being able to connect it to something and this for years?" It exemplifies what an affect means in the real. It is useful to remind ourselves of Lacan's definition, as already quoted: "the real is lawless". In this case, it demonstrates via the impossibility of establishing the least explanatory connection, that what is missing here is the possibility of giving sense to this bad mood.

It is the issue Lacan is addressing by other means: "this we call moroseness, or equally, moodiness. Is this a sin, a grain of madness, or a true touch of the real?"[16] Indeed, in the case described above, for the subject there is no hold, no possibility to fragment the bad mood, it falls onto the subject. It is the return of the affect in the real, as was the case with the return of the signifier in the real. Lacan demonstrates it in a paradigmatic way with the voice in the hallucination. The voice is a medium of signifier. It is a localized signifier which takes a pure form. The example described putting moroseness at the center; this is to be inscribed in what's today known as "the depressive states", which correspond to a trans-nosographic denomination. Depression, as this case demonstrates, is not solely a reaction to a loss. There are depressions which are bound to a subjective despondency without it becoming a case of melancholy, and without any reason to explain it. Therefore, someone who has had difficulties without any reason gives us an indication of what could be the manifestation of "*L'Achose*". It would be the return of an affect within the real. Therefore, the psychotic subject's problematics regards the fact that he does not accommodate the Thing [*la Chose*] on the Other's side, since the Other is on his side. That's why he prefers to believe in himself rather than in the Other. For sure, there are sometimes psychotic subjects who give the impression of believing in the Other, except that when the Other responds, the subject tirelessly replies: "It's not that." Therefore, eventually, it is a trap, a strategy addressed to the Other; basically, whether he responds or not, it's secondary, the subject won't believe it.

All this to nuance the idea that one should always find the conviction on the psychotic side. Sometimes the psychotic's question, which must remain unanswered, is an effect of the unbelief in the Other, and it may take the form of a conviction. In a way, in psychosis the subject-supposed-to-know [*le sujet-supposé-savoir*] is a kind of dismissal of the Other even before that one has been constituted. From then, the question is: how may a psychotic subject choose an analyst as a partner? One may choose a partner to be assisted, to be accompanied, and even request the Other for guidance on the unconscious warnings. In this case, the psychotic subject makes his analyst a partner of his cause. And the analyst, if he decides to take this place, must consent to remain there, as long as it takes. Yet, this position of transference, wherein the analyst is placed by the psychotic subject, includes distinctions to be made when the analysand is a schizophrenic subject.

The case in schizophrenia

There is certainly a problem in defining what is meant by a schizophrenic subject. We can see it each time there is a debate between psychiatrists and psychoanalysts. For psychiatry, the diagnostic of schizophrenia rests on three terms: disorganization, delirious ideas, and deficit. Actually, these three terms – it is more subtle with delirious ideas – converge around one topic, which is the notion of deficit. The Lacanian clinic takes another option. It excludes the dimension of deficit yet perceives the invention as possible. It does not start from a clinical term, admittedly fundamental, that is to say the schizophrenic negativity. Thus, this clinical option bases itself on what is possible to obtain from the original data, but also aims to produce what was not there before the analysis. It's why one says with Lacan that it is an analytical procedure. In that meaning, from the analytical perspective, there is a change of perspective in the clinic of schizophrenia from Lacan's sharpest definition of it when he poses: "the so-called schizophrenic is specified as being taken beyond the help of any established discourse".[17] Besides, when Lacan argues that the schizophrenic is not caught in a speech, we deduce that the other types of psychosis may be.

In other words, the schizophrenic is in the language; he speaks, he talks to the other, but he enters no discourse. It is a reason why he can't speak to an analyst. To not enter a discourse is not necessarily a deficit. It can be an originality. To be outside any discourses is a special subjective position. It is an originality in the sense that it sets someone apart. If the schizophrenic addresses an analyst, while he remains banned from discourses, therefore as well from analytic discourses, it is because he has found a partner in line with his freedom. Indeed, it is with a partner being as free as he is that he may aspire to find a place in the world, even if it is not a place within the discourses. Thus, and again, the case-based clinic has to be kept in mind to practice the analysis, where precisely the need to find one's way via the exception is checked.

Let's revert to the definition of schizophrenia given by a psychiatry focused on the German term of *Spaltung*. It tells of a dissociation in the operation of associations. It's interesting, since the fundamental rule of psychoanalysis is free association. It indirectly highlights the reason why free association is not a diffluent process. The reason is that to give to the analysand the freedom to associate does not lead to the loss of what constitutes the axis of associations. The speech, even the free one, is governed by what establishes the subject's structure. A dissociation, on the contrary, results in an alteration in the operation of associations. It's the case with *Spaltung*, a term Freud made use of, borrowed from Janet. Janet's idea is that a subject is having thoughts and that there are thoughts or secondary images. This proposition has shaped Freud's idea to make use of the notion of hypnoid state, as constitutive of hysteria. It is about a state where consciousness is confused. At the beginning, Freud's idea is that it is inappropriate to speak of a *Spaltung* within consciousness but of a *Spaltung* within psyche. Therefore, it's already clear as soon as the "Preliminary Communication" (1893), then in "Studies of Hysteria" (1895), where Freud outlines the Lacanian idea of a subject afflicted by a constitutive division. He speaks of a dissociation within psyche. It was in his early works about hysteria; he makes use of the same term of *Spaltung* to mention the fetishism phenomenon. Namely an essential idea, conscious, and then something which appears as minor to the subject, is this idea that somewhere there is the need to rely on fetishism. Bleuler, for his part, makes use of the term *Spaltung* to indicate a disorganization, a disaggregation, a loss of unity, and to specify therefore the schizophrenia. We see from these developments how in Lacan may emerge what will become the notion of subjective division as being the essence of neurosis. The neurotic subject is divided. Then Lacan will consider the existence of a "*schize*" [split], and there precisely he involves the term of *Spaltung*, which he was keeping for psychosis. By the end of Freud's work, the term of *Spaltung* has been translated into French as "*clivage*" [cleavage] and the literature in English made use of it to define psychosis. Lacan chose to make use of Freud's notion of psyche dissociation, meaning within the psyche a division correlating to neurosis, and the "*schize*" [split] to speak about psychosis, while English authors, in particular Bion, use the term of *splitting* as being specific to schizophrenia. This is how Bion refers to the attack against the link or the break of the link. And then in France, Racamier, in the IPA, evokes the dis-objectivization, then retains the psychiatric terms of psychic disorganization, namely the break of the link between two objects.

For Lacan, in schizophrenia, the subject who does not embody a discourse is a subject for whom "all of the symbolic is real",[18] meaning that it is a subject who's living the real. For a subject organized like this, there is no relation to the "object a"; he is in the real. That is precisely like a melancholic subject right at the time of the passage to the act, he identifies himself to the object; therefore, if the identification is with the object, it means that the subject is the object, consequently here there is no fantasy. Again, in psychosis that's a proof of the dissolution of the distance to the object, which is obvious at the time of the passage to the act. There is the other example from Lacan to which I already referred, about The Wolf Man, where he says that it is "pure fantasy", emphasizing that the wolf's fascinated gaze, "is the subject himself".[19] We return to the term of *distance*. When the subject is the object, there is no more distance. It's confirmed with the clinical cases, this absence of mediation going through the fantasy, while in paranoia, there exists a possibility of mediation. And when Lacan poses that for the paranoiac there is a possibility to adjourn to an indeterminate future, it is to connect the subjective position to a temporality which wouldn't be exclusively the instant, while the schizophrenic is in the instant, then in a wholly disconnected way *arises* the following instant; there is no before and there is no after. Therefore, actually, when we evoke a subject's delusional dimension – I speak about its therapeutic virtues – what Freud named the attempt of healing is a delusion which is at the service of an accommodation of the subject being-in-the-world, based on a fantasy. From this point, it's interesting to return to the paranoia. That's what Freud states in "A Child is Being Beaten", when he makes a demonstration about fantasy in neurosis, he concludes: "I should not be surprised if it were one day possible to prove that the same phantasy is the basis of the delusional litigiousness of paranoia".[20]

In one of his ultimate definitions of paranoia, Lacan argues that the paranoiac subject identifies the *jouissance* where the Other resides. With this formulation, we get the impression that eventually each subject possesses a dimension slightly paranoiac. Actually, his self includes a paranoiac dimension, in the sense that the subject's self necessarily constitutes itself out of the Other, and therefore for any subject there exists this interrogation: what does the Other want? The paranoiac, he concludes before the question arises. To pose the definition of paranoia in terms of identification of the Other's *jouissance*, is already another use of the term *identification*: it's not the subject who is having an identification, it's not to identify oneself to one's symptom, but it's to identify the *jouissance* as where the Other resides. To identify the *jouissance* as where the Other resides is an attribution, it's an attempt to localize an initiative, the location of emission of *jouissance*, and to have the conviction that it's coming from the Other. Therefore, with this wording to localize the *jouissance* to where the Other resides, there exists at the same time a dimension linked to the desire, in the sense that the subject sustains himself with this dimension where exists an Other who wants the subject's *jouissance*, and therefrom that one adjusts his subjective position. Schreber, in regard of God, adjusts his position, he poses the *jouissance* as coming from God – divine *jouissance* – but at the same time it enables him to fix his own position.

Let's also consider the delusions of jealousy: as we have said, Lacan puts it like this in *The Formations of the Unconscious*: "as psychotic, I try to establish in the Other this desire".[21] What does it mean? It's related to desire, it's the subject beginning with Freud's formulation posed as a modality of negation of a unique formulation "myself, being a man, I love a man". That's the formulation we find in regards to Schreber, from which Freud applies three grammatical forms to evoke simultaneously the delusion of persecution, the delusion of jealousy, or the erotomania. The delusion of jealousy is characterized by bringing to life another one who is feeling a desire for someone else. That is a delusional process: at fault for having his own desire, the subject tries to assert that the other has a desire for someone else, but it's such a fantasy that he'll organize all his actions in life from this formulation. He knows – in his opinion – that someone else is desired, to understand it, time has to be abolished, and the very moment of seeing sticks to the very moment to conclude.

Let's take the erotomania. I mentioned earlier Lacan's phrase from "Television": "A woman meets the man within psychosis". It's the erotomania counterpart, since a woman that assumes "the other loves me", makes out of this partner an exceptional man, and in which case she meets *the* Man. She meets the exceptional man, a man who's not like the others, a man who avoids the castration. Whereas it's everyone's experience, the hysteric subject first – except during the "*coup de foudre*" phase – and right after, that a disappointment will occur, linked to the lack in the other and an effect of the encounter with the man's castration. It's why following the initial fascinations, what's appearing is the enumeration of what is missing in the other. Therefore, to believe that *the* Man exists, one has to possess a dose of madness. To come across *the* Man, it's to ensure that the sexual intercourse does exist. In other words, what the hysteric subject is complaining about, is that there is no man being worthy. Yet precisely, in psychosis, to come across the man, means to come across *the* uncastrated Man, *the* Man in capital letter, the one to whom nothing's missing, but to be able to choose him, there must be a whole apparatus both of images and language to build up a figure of who that man is. Therefore, it falls under fantasy! The question is, why does the erotomaniac brings into life this exceptional man? For if this man exists and "he chooses me", then "consequently, I become the exceptional woman". It's precisely why there is a converging point between the proposition "come across *the* Man" in psychosis and another proposition put forward by Lacan in "l'Etourdit", which in psychosis is "push-to-the-woman" [*pousse-à-la-femme*].[22] For, as a woman, to personify the exception, there has to be a fantasy. Thus, we understand the megalomaniac dimension of this fantasy. It enables the personification of a woman out of the phallic measure [*la mesure phallique*]. For her, it's not enough to be unique for someone. To a set, she must become the missing one. We clearly distinguish that the use of fantasy differs from what, in neurosis, the subject makes of it. In that case, the fantasy may sometimes be used to avoid the encounter with the real; we frequently say it, the subject prefers to dream. For sure, to dream is not the same as being confronted to one's drive. The subject satisfies himself with his fantasy, even if paradoxically fantasy drives him to remain unsatisfied. But the fantasy is what leads the subject towards the quest for the object of satisfaction. The fantasy provides a framework which places the subject within the phallic limits.

Therefore, I revert to the use of fantasy. If we consider neurosis, it's what Lacan wrote as S ...a. The stamp indicates at the same time a relation between conjunction and disjunction. That is to say that the relation between the subject and his "object a", the cause of his desire, is a relation between things which fit together and things which are disjointed, with nothing absolute in all this. What we can perceive in psychosis and that is coherent with Lacan's formulation: the psychotic subject "has his cause in his pocket".[23] To have the "object a" in the pocket, means that one is having a direct relation to the object. There is no conjunction/disjunction, there is no articulation; the subject has a close relationship to the object, it's why there is such ease to move to action, to – using the formulation above – overstep things. If the psychotic subject oversteps, it's because of a lack of articulation, of conjunction/disjunction, and things are being played absolutely. Therefore, there is a lack of relationship, an abolition of the distance. It's why Lacan applies to this case the "*causa sui*", namely when the subject is his own issue, and does not situate the cause of desire on the Other's side. In this sense he personifies the free man.

Return to fantasy

In psychanalysis, to think about the subject, is to think about the subject of the unconscious. The subjective division is because of the surprise being triggered by the unconscious formations. The subject is divided between his intention, and what comes from the unconscious, namely missteps, dreams, slips of the tongue. That is this logic which enables Lacan to differentiate the subject and the self, which is translated into what is remaining as an enunciation beneath the subject's statements. At this point, it becomes essential to identify what is not grasped in the subject's statements. There is what a subject does not say and what he does not know, sometimes after the analysis is well under way, but it's what determines his actions and his thoughts. And precisely there, Lacan in accordance with Freud situates the fantasy. The fantasy is what a subject is using to accede to his satisfaction. Of course, there is the drive-based satisfaction, but to accede to it the subject builds up an apparatus which enables him to achieve this satisfaction. It's why it's interesting to seize Freud's formulation: "phantasy has the value of a fact". It means that someone may be satisfied via the satisfaction of fantasy, which besides may also include a dissatisfaction. For analysis it's a crucial question: how may a subject give up the satisfaction of fantasy and switch to another form of satisfaction? For the subject, Lacan's thesis is that fantasy is an alternative to the real. Therefore, it works as a cover and it's all the more a reason not to let it go, since it serves as a guideline to the subject, and in analysis it's what he'll have to deal with. Underlying the fantasy is situated the most intimate core, the subject's Being.

Lacan formulated it in a different way when he mentions, as we highlighted, that fantasy is an axiom. In logic, an *axiom* is a term which indicates the premise of a phrase which adjusts a behavior. Therefore, there is a grammar of fantasy, already noted by Freud in his text "A Child is Being Beaten", which emphasizes how a phrase constitutes the basis onto which a subject sustains himself, and which adjusts the whole of his behaviors. Actually, this axiom is an attempt to give an account of the subject's *jouissance*, simultaneously to explain it, to justify it, and to make sure to accommodate the subject to this *jouissance*. Therefore, when we pose the subject's division, we pose that something is also beyond surprise by the unconscious. We assume a loss of *jouissance*, an effect of language. This loss has to be recovered somewhere. It's where Lacan lodges fantasy, what he has written as: S ...*a*, the *a* resuming the lost part of *jouissance*. In other words, fantasy is structured as an attempt through recurring behaviors to recover the lost *jouissance*. Therefore, it's a mechanism of compensation, of adjustment. When the "object *a*" finds its place in fantasy and it works, then in this case we may say that for the subject, fantasy is truly acting as the real. It does not mean that fantasy is a pure real. It's why Lacan was able to say that in an analysis, there must be a traversal of fantasy. What is intuiting the idea that there must be an axiom, is the fact that the "object *a*" is within a dependence to the linguistic articulation. Thus, *a* is the remainder once the subject has been pervaded by language. It's what leaves the subject being dependent on the way language has traversed him. The question is how the treatment finds its way of aiming at the traversal of fantasy. Here, the notion of cut is essential. As Lacan says: "the cut made by the signifying chain is the only cut that verifies the structure of the subject as a discontinuity in the real".[24]

While we could assume that an analysis is done in order to give a sense which escapes, a sense in addition, there what it means, according to this proposal, is to generate a discontinuity; which requires making cuts in the signifying chain. That's something else than to give sense. So, what's interesting in the text "The Subversion of the Subject and the Dialectic of Desire", is that immediately after, Lacan evokes Mallarmé. It's not the first time he quotes him. He already does it with regard to the same question, but to say something else. In his text "The Function and Field of Speech and Language in Psychoanalysis", he formulates: "the analyst's art must, on the contrary, involve suspending the subject's certainties until their final mirages have been consumed", then he adds: "and it is in the subject's discourse that their dissolution must be punctuated".[25] At the time, there was already the notion that an analysis works to enable mirages to be consumed. We already notice in this idea that by the end of his teachings he's going to pose that truth is lying. The idea somehow was already there, the mirage which must consume itself. So, when he evokes it through the following phrases, he summons Mallarmé who compares the common use of language to the exchange of a coin whose obverse and reverse bear nothing but eroded faces "and which people pass from hand to hand 'in silence'".[26] Here is precisely where Lacan ends his phrase, saying: "it is, therefore, a propitious punctuation that gives meaning to the subject's discourse".[27]

Lacan had the idea that it was about producing, via the interpretation, a new sense which would come as a happy punctuation. The happy punctuation, at the time, was the aim of the analytical interpretation. Lacan likewise refers thereby, to how the analyst must put an end to the session, and in another way than by the elapsed time. The happy punctuation is to put a full stop where the subject had left some suspension points and where a subject had put a comma. When Lacan resumes the same reference to Mallarmé, years later in "The Subversion of the Subject and the Dialectic of Desire", it is not to link it to the happy punctuation. Lacan again evokes the idea of "the worn coinage Mallarmé speaks of that is passed from hand to hand 'in silence'".[28] This time it's to tell us that we must return to the function of the cut in the discourse. In other words, what is passing from hand to hand "in silence" sends us back to the analyst's silence, to something which goes by the speech, but simultaneously which must be spent in the use of the speech. It also indicates what the analyst's place must be with regard to the discourse in the session, and there precisely is introduced the idea "that discourse in an analytic session is worthwhile only insofar as it stumbles, or even interrupts itself".[29] Lacan adds:

> Were not the session itself instituted as a break in a false discourse, that is, in what discourse realizes when it becomes empty as speech, when it is no more that the worn coinage Mallarmé speaks of that is passed from hand to hand "in silence"?[30]

In other words, the fundamental question Lacan introduces instead of the "happy punctuation", aims to generate in the subject's discourse something which stumbles, something which interrupts itself. He thereby returns to the question: how to put an end to the session? But this time his idea is that one does not put an end to it by giving a new sense. The idea is to produce a rupture in the discourse. The cut Lacan is making use of is the rod between signifier and signified. In this context, the cut is to leave the subject with the signifier so that he stops asking himself: "But what does it mean?" This question endlessly repeated makes the analysis endless. The endless analysis is made of a quest for more meaning. Then the essential is not so much what the subject is saying, but where he ends it, and he may stop spontaneously or not. From there, what is fundamental is how the analyst makes an end to the subject's discourse. The idea is that the termination of the session, as Lacan resumes it, is done to enable the subject to understand that the discourse he is in composes the mask which overlaps his Being's essence. It is the reason why Lacan posed that fantasy is in lieu of the real. That's also why he has been able to pose this distinction between signifier and signified occurring by the cut, that the analysis must reveal it since it's there that the truth of this relationship appears. Even more precisely, he indicates that "analysis reveals the truth of this relationship by making holes in meaning the determinants of its discourse".[31] According to this conception, it is about an orientation which aims at the subject's real, and which is opposite to an objective aimed at giving more sense. It is rather about making visible that someone's true Being lies where the hole of sense [le trou du sens] is forged, and therefrom is formulated and structured that the subject will rely on this hole of sense to found his discourse. Therefore, this formulation displays the paradoxical character of analysis. When the analysands, and even the analysts, begin the control and call for sense, they look for the meaning of symptoms, they seek answers to the enigmas of actions. So, what is the analyst's answer? If we follow Lacan, the analyst's statement sustains itself on this: truth arises provided that within sense, holes are being drilled.

The impossible to bear

A practice which aims the hole within the sense assumes that the sense, given by the subject to his existence's enigmas, are myths produced to better withstand what for each of us is the impossible to bear. It makes me revert to that formulation which appears in the "Opening of the Clinical Section" conference where Lacan answers what defines the analytical clinic, that it is "the real insofar as it is impossible to bear".[32] This phrase is important since Lacan formulates it for the first time, emending what he had already stated, since a few years earlier, he had provided a definition of real: "the impossible is the real". So, was it the same thing to say that "the impossible is the real" as to say "the real insofar as it is impossible to bear"?

The impossible as a real refers to the logic. That's the real as it is the emergence of an impasse in formalization. When we can't apply a logical framework to something, we can run into trouble and this logical trouble is the real. The real in logic is what we can't bring into the logic. It is why Lacan said: "which does not cease to not write itself";[33] in other words, it's a symbolic outcast.[34] The symbolic is the attempt to capture something, but there's always something which makes an obstacle. That's what we are unable to write: a real, logical, which escapes to the signifying machine, therefore to the symbolic. The example is the formulation "there is no sexual relation". It is a logical formulation saying nothing about what's going on between two sexual beings. Therefore, it is a logical real, that is to say that the sexual relation can't be written. "The impossible to bear" is from another register. If the real as an impossible is linked to logic and to mathematics, now the question is about what one means by "to bear it". This introduces the subject's dimension. The real linked to logic does not fall under the palpable. On the other hand, when one says that there is something impossible to bear, it's because it is tangible, and there it affects the body.

For something to be impossible to bear, it must be so for someone. Therefore, there we are in the subject, we are in someone's dimension taking the weight upon oneself, the pain of something. That is to say that to bear something, there must be a matter of body. Therefore, the impossible to bear is a way of saying: "my body does not bear it". And even when it's a thought which is unbearable, it's the same; the body is always affected when it's about the unbearable. When Lacan suggests his proposition "the analytical clinic is the real insofar as it is impossible to bear", does he refer to the analysand or to the analyst? It may be that an analyst in his practice comes across an impossible to bear. It's sometimes the case when the analysand's "spoken words" [les dits], which are not supposed to interfere in the treatment, affect the analyst's fantasy. This leads occasionally to anxiety. In any case, when there is something unbearable on the analyst's side, it is because it's appropriate that he resumes an analysis to adjust his relationship to his desire to be an analyst. Therefore, the impossible to bear is essentially in reference to the analysand. It's the reason why he resorts to analysis, and that's always something to explore.

Why is someone applying for an analysis today and not at another time? The specific reason is that he suddenly came across something which is unbearable. For example, a subject who ignores the existence of death and around him someone dies; it illustrates what may be unbearable. Likewise, an experience of unexpected *jouissance*, that may be an unbearable encounter. That may be something which has always existed, and one day there is what precipitates it and it becomes unbearable. In a way, that applies to what Lacan said about Dora. In *The Psychosis* and *The Formations of the Unconscious*, Lacan poses that, for Dora, life was acceptable up to the time when the "situation decompensates". It means that at some point, there is an unbearable which becomes present. It's the sign of a failure of fantasy. The fantasy, whose subject used it at some point to overlap the real, tears itself, making things unbearable. Here, I resume why Lacan said that "object *a*" has a consistent logic. It's the relationship to this "object *a*" which means that the subject is holding up in his existence. It is a consistent logic because the "object *a*" is able to assume the subject's lack. There, where lack is staying, the "object *a*" localizes it. It's how the subject can deal with the lack until something appears as being unbearable.

The question is about fantasy in psychosis. Lacan is explicit in his text "Direction of the Treatment and the Principles of Its Power", where he makes use of the formulation "usage of phantasy in neurosis, perversion or psychosis".[35] Then we may add the whole of Schreber's articulations about becoming "God's wife", which must be considered as fantasy. In the same way, we have the already evoked formulation of Lacan's in "Television": "woman encounters man in psychosis". It means that in a number of cases of psychosis, fantasy exists to encounter *the* Man. On the other hand, it's true as Lacan said, that there is a use of fantasy in psychosis which is different from the use in neurosis, owing to the relationship to the "object *a*" which is not the same. Must we deduce that there is no possible interpretation in psychosis? One may argue, *a minima*, that there is an interpretation which aims to introduce a distance with psychotic phenomena. Therefore, the cut in psychosis, is not to display the hole of sense [*le trou du sens*], because the risk would be to leave the subject as close as possible to the real, and then a passage to the act could happen. On the other hand, it is possible to interpret, and even to make a cut in some cases where delusional ideas lead the subject to a pure *jouissance*, and are not at his service to protect him from the real. And there, there must be a cut. The aim is therefore, to cut the subject where he is standing on a deadly slope. Therefore, in this perspective, the function of the cut would be to enable the ordering of the subject's delusion to allow him to orient himself, and thus distinguish between a delusion which could be used as a prosthesis and a delusion which could turn to a dimension of persecution. Therefore, when we say with Freud, that delusion is an attempt to heal, it's too vast a formulation. There are delusions which certainly protect, but there are delusions which are on the verge of being a breach of *jouissance*, and there the analyst has an ethical responsibility: these delusions have to be cut off. Sometimes it is necessary to limit a delusion, as long as the analyst does not come to embody the breach, for the risk then is to become the figure of an Other persecutor.

Notes

1 Lacan, J., « Propos sur la causalité physique », in *Écrits*, Paris, Le Seuil, 1966, p. 177. ("Presentation on Psychical Causality", *Écrits*, New York and London, W.W. Norton and Company, 2002, p. 145. Translation by B. Fink in collaboration with H. Fink.)
2 Lacan, J., *Le Séminaire, Livre XVI, d'Un Autre à l'autre*, p. 332. (*From an Other to the other: The Seminar of Jacques Lacan, Book XVI*, p. 288. Translation by B. Fink.)
3 Lacan, J., *Le Séminaire, Livre XVI, d'Un Autre à l'autre*, p. 332. (*From an Other to the other: The Seminar of Jacques Lacan, Book XVI*, p. 288. Translation by B. Fink.)
4 Lacan, J., « Proposition du 9 octobre 1967 sur le psychanalyste de l'Ecole », in *Autres écrits*, Paris, Le Seuil, 2001 p. 247. ("Proposition of 9 October 1967 on the Psychoanalyst of the School", p. 4. Translation by R. Grigg.)
5 Lacan, J., *Le Séminaire, Livre VIII, Le transfert*, p. 12. (*The Seminar of Jacques Lacan, Book VIII, Transference*, p. 3. Translation by C. Gallagher.)

6   Lacan, J., *Le Séminaire, Livre III, Les Psychoses*, Paris, le Seuil, 1981, leçon du 25 janvier 1956, p. 121. (*The Seminar of Jacques Lacan, Book III, The Psychosis*, W.W. Norton and Company. p. 106. Translation by R. Grigg.)

7   Lacan, J., *Le Séminaire, Livre III, Les Psychoses*, Paris, le Seuil, 1981, leçon du 25 janvier 1956, p. 120. (*The Seminar of Jacques Lacan, Book III, The Psychosis*, W.W. Norton and Company, p. 106. Translation by R. Grigg.)

8   Freud, S., *Sigmund Freud's Letters to Wilhem Fliess (1887–1902)*, Basic Books, New York 1954. Draft H, 24-I-95, p. 113. Translation by Eris Mosbacher and James Strachey.

9   Lacan, J., *Le Séminaire, Livre VI, Les formations de l'inconscient*, Paris, Le Seuil, 1998, p. 482. (*The Seminar of Jacques Lacan, Book VI, The Formations of the Unconscious*, W.W. Norton and Company. p. 445. Translation by C. Gallagher.)

10 Lacan, J., *Le Séminaire, Livre XXIII, Le sinthome*, Paris, Le Seuil, 2005, p. 77 and pp. 87–89. (*The Seminar of Jacques Lacan, Book XXIII, The Sinthome*, Polity, Cambridge and New York, 2016, p. 72. Translation by A.R. Price.)

11 Lacan, J., *Le Séminaire, Livre VII, L'éthique de la psychanalyse*, p. 329. (My translation.)

12 Lacan, J., *Le Séminaire, Livre VII, L'éthique de la psychanalyse*, p. 362. (My translation.)

13 Lacan, J., *"The Ethics of Psychoanalysis" The Seminar of Jacques Lacan: Book VII*. London and New York, Routledge, 2008, p. 283. Translated by Dennis Porter.

14 Lacan, J., Séminaire XXIV "L'Insu que sait de l'une bévue s'aile à mourre", séance du 16 Novembre 1976, inédit.Seminar XXIV, "L'Insu que sait de l'une bévue s'aile à mourre".Wednesday 16 november 1976. p. 3. Translated by Cormac Gallagher.

15 Lacan, J., « Conférence aux psychiatres », 1967, inédit. (Conference to Psychiatrists.)

16 Lacan, J., « Télévision » in *Autres écrits*, p. 527. ("Television", W.W. Norton and Company, New York and London, p. 24. Translation by D. Hollier, R. Krauss and A. Michelson.)

17 Lacan, J., « L'étourdit » in *Autres écrits*, p. 474. ("L'Etourdit", p. 18. Translation by J.W. Stone.)

18 Lacan, J., « Introduction au commentaire de Jean Hyppolite sur la « *Verneinung* » de Freud », in *Écrits*, Paris, Le Seuil, 1966, p. 392. ("Response to Jean Hyppolite's Commentary on Freud's 'Verneinung', *Écrits*, New York and London, W. W. Norton and Company, 2002, p. 327. Translation by B. Fink in collaboration with H. Fink.)

19 Lacan, J., *Le Séminaire, Livre XI, Les quatre concepts fondamentaux de la psychanalyse*, p. 227. (*The Four Fundamental Concepts of Psychoanalysis, From Interpretation to the Transference: The Seminar of Jacques Lacan, Book XI*, W.W. Norton and Company, New York and London, p. 251. Translation by A. Sheridan.)

20 Freud, S., "On the Teaching of Psycho-Analysis in Universities" (1919), in *The Standard Edition of the Complete Psychological Works of Sigmund Freud*, 17, London, The Hogarth Press, 169–174.

21 Lacan, J., Séminaire V "Les formations de l'inconscient", Paris, Le Seuil, 1998, p. 481. (Seminar V, "The Formations of the Unconscious", p. 445. Translated by Cormac Gallagher.)

22 Lacan, J., "L'étourdit", Scilicet 4 Editions du Seuil, 1973, pp. 5–52, repris dans *Autres écrits*, Le Seuil, 2001, pp. 449–495. "L'Etourdit", p. 50. Translated by Cormac Gallagher. "Push-to-the-woman" here is the only available translation and means to transform oneself from man to woman in the Schreber case.

23 Lacan, J., « Conférence aux psychiatres », 1967, inédit. Conference to Psychiatrists.

24 Lacan, J., « Subversion du sujet et dialectique du désir dans l'inconscient freudien », in *Écrits*, Paris, Le Seuil, 1966, p. 801. ("The Subversion of the Subject and the Dialectic of Desire", *Écrits*, New York and London, W.W. Norton and Company, 2002, p. 678. Translation by B. Fink in collaboration with H. Fink.)

25 Lacan, J., « Fonction et champ de la parole et du language en psychanalyse » In *Écrits*, Paris, Le Seuil, 1966, p. 251. ("The Function and Field of Speech and Language in Psychoanalysis", *Écrits*, New York and London, W.W. Norton and Company, 2002, p. 209. Translation by B. Fink in collaboration with H. Fink.)

26 Lacan, J., « Fonction et champ de la parole et du language en psychanalyse » In *Écrits*, Paris, Le Seuil, 1966, p. 251. ("The Function and Field of Speech and Language in Psychoanalysis", *Écrits*, New York and London, W.W. Norton and Company, 2002, p. 209. Translation by B. Fink in collaboration with H. Fink.)

27 Lacan, J., « Fonction et champ de la parole et du language en psychanalyse » In *Écrits*, Paris, Le Seuil, 1966, p. 252. ("The Function and Field of Speech and Language in Psychoanalysis", *Écrits*, New York and London, W.W. Norton and Company, 2002, p. 209. Translation by B. Fink in collaboration with H. Fink.)

28 Lacan, J., « Subversion du sujet et dialectique du désir dans l'inconscient freudien » In *Écrits*, Paris, Le Seuil, 1966, p. 801. ("The Subversion of the Subject and the Dialectic of Desire", *Écrits*, New York and London, W.W. Norton and Company, 2002, p. 678. Translation by B. Fink in collaboration with H. Fink.)

29 Lacan, J., « Fonction et champ de la parole et du language en psychanalyse » In *Écrits*, Paris, Le Seuil, 1966, p. 251. ("The Function and Field of Speech and Language in Psychoanalysis", *Écrits*, New York and London, W.W. Norton and Company, 2002, p. 209. Translation by B. Fink in collaboration with H. Fink.)

30 Lacan, J., « Subversion du sujet et dialectique du désir dans l'inconscient freudien » In *Écrits*, Paris, Le Seuil, 1966, p. 801. ("The Subversion of the Subject and the Dialectic of Desire", *Écrits*, New York and London, W.W. Norton and Company, 2002, p. 678. Translation by B. Fink in collaboration with H. Fink.)

31 Lacan, J., « Subversion du sujet et dialectique du désir dans l'inconscient freudien » In *Écrits*, Paris, Le Seuil, 1966, p. 801. ("The Subversion of the Subject and the Dialectic of Desire", *Écrits*, New York and London, W.W. Norton and Company, 2002, p. 678. Translation by B. Fink in collaboration with H. Fink.)

32 Lacan, J., « Ouverture à la section clinique », *Ornicar?*, n°9, 1977, pp. 7–14. (Opening of the Clinical Section. p. 7. Translation by R. Groome and Q and A by R.G. Klein.)

33 Lacan, J. "Introduction à l'édition allemande d'un premier volume des *Écrits*", Paris, Le Seuil, 1975, p. 637.("Introduction to a first volume of the Ecrits [Walter Verlag]", Scilicet, 1975, n°5, p. 5. Translated by J.W. Stone.)

34 Lacan, J. "Introduction à l'édition allemande d'un premier volume des *Écrits*", Paris, Le Seuil, 1975, p. 637.("Introduction to a first volume of the Ecrits [Walter Verlag]", Scilicet, 1975, n°5, p. 5. Translated by J.W. Stone.)

35 Lacan, J. Séminaire XXIV "La direction de la cure et les principes de son pouvoir", *Écrits*. Paris, Le Seuil, 1975, p. 637. (*Direction of the Treatment and the Principles of Its Power*, New York and London, W.W Norton & Company, p. 532. Translated by B. Fink in collaboration with H. Fink and R. Grigg.)

Chapter 5

The Symptom of End

The singular fantasy

Is there not a contradiction or a paradox in Lacan's formulation posed about the future of symptom in analysis: "might it be or might it not be, to identify oneself, a kind of distance, to identify oneself to one's symptom?"[1] To be identified seems incompatible with the idea of keeping a certain distance, or else one is not completely identified. It is therefore appropriate to return to what we mean by this question from the end of his teaching. Let's resume his text: "The Direction of the Treatment and the Principles of its Power" where he poses the future of the identifications in the treatment through a passive form, since he declares "the identifications are denounced".[2] To say it like that is something else than to say that the analyst denounces the identifications. "The identifications are denounced" means that in the course of the analysis, by the interpretations – not necessarily directly – the identifications appear to the subject as coming from the Other. Therefore, there is a disclosure which occurs. On the other hand, if one is identified, one does not notice it. It's the paradoxical use of the term *identification* regarding the end of the analysis, for as we said, one considers the analysis as an experience of de-identification.

Why do we use the term identification to speak about what is expected as the final result of the analysis? When we say identification, we must start from Lacan's definition introduced in "The Identification": it seeks to "remove a signifier to the Other". That's what is denounced during the treatment, these are signifiers coming from the Other. It already compels us to differentiate between the identification and the "as if". The latter is specific to psychosis as a behavior in which we borrow a behavior from the other. To do as the other does is not the same thing as to remove a signifier to the Other. If we start from this formulation regarding the identification, it's true that there is a paradox in making use of the formulation "to identify oneself to the symptom", since the symptom is not the other, it's something which belongs to oneself. It's why Lacan does not precisely make use of the term *identification* to speak of the end of the analysis, but preferably he

DOI: 10.4324/9781003568315-6

makes use of the expression "to identify oneself". "To identify oneself to the symptom" supposes that you acknowledge that it's coming out of you, that you are precisely "that", that is to say the most intimate nucleus, therefore the subject's name.

Then, Lacan adds these formulations: "while taking some insurance" and "a kind of distance". The idea of insurance means that the subject is informed that "that" is his symptom; and at the same time "taking some insurance" is to make sure that each time, the subject knows which part of his symptom is involved in what's happening to him in the world. Besides, to refer to "a kind of distance" supposes not to exhibit excessively this symptom; one knows it's one's symptom, no need to assert it, nor to hide behind it by telling oneself that it's up to you to fend for, since "it's my symptom". Therefore, to keep "a kind of distance", is to be in a dimension of know-how with his symptom without infiltrating the relationship to the other. I consider that, this way, the obvious paradox may be resolved between, on the one hand, identifying oneself, and on the other, knowing that one should pay attention to not letting the symptom make too much damage around oneself.

It is true that Lacan posed the end of analysis in terms of crossing the identifications level, which is the equivalent of posing the de-identification. But Lacan does not stop there, since de-identification includes an "I am not like the others", therefore a dimension both of distance towards oneself but also towards the others. That's a distance to consider the other as a model. It is "no more model", no more ideal either. So, once the ancient models fall apart, one should realize that for a subject there is nothing which could function as a new ideal. Yet, what we may observe in analysis is that there exists a slope in subjects, which, once a number of identifications and even ideals are moving, generates new identifications. Therefore, it's not enough that ancient identifications fall apart and that even the infantile ideal plummets, it is necessary to verify that new identifications and ideals did not come instead. The idea of traversing the identifications level includes a dimension of partition, but it does not tell us how the subject is living it. And that is precisely Lacan's novelty. We say that psychoanalysts refuse the evaluation, but it's not entirely accurate. Lacan in this regard describes a real program showing how to evaluate the analysis by the way the subject lives his relationship with the drive. It's not enough by the end of an analysis to be separated from the Other's desire, nor to assume an original desire, and what Lacan emphasizes as a program for post-analysis is how a subject lives the drive.

It's very important to note that, with regard to the mechanism Lacan invented to evaluate the analyst's desire, he repeatedly makes use of the term *selection*. It seems amazing for someone who said that to occupy the analyst's place, there is an authorization coming out of oneself. Simultaneously, Lacan sticks to the idea of a selection. It means that there is a logical need to assert that the analyst authorizes himself. Lacan produces a procedure of selection based upon an evaluation of what is the analyst's desire on the basis of his act, but he says that it's up to the psychoanalytic school to single out the cases where the analyst's desire seems proven. Therefore, there exists an exigency to demonstrate how the advent of the analyst's desire is the result of a change in the relation to the drive. In this sense, Lacan makes use of a series of grammatical formulas regarding the drive, which follow the model of fantasy "a child is being beaten" identified by Freud. It's illustrated in the subject's relation to the drive-based objects; leading to: "we're being devoured", "we're fucking bored", "we're being fooled", "we're making ourselves heard". These are variations of the relationship to the objects of the drive: oral, anal, scopic [*scopique*], voice. And it displays a visible incidence in the change performed by the analysis. Thus, a subject, after a number of years of analysis, notices for example, that eventually all he did in his life was to accommodate himself to this drive-based relationship. That is to say, that there was for him something which satisfied itself, even if he complained about it. When we evoke how a subject lives the drive after the analysis, it's not only to be able to acknowledge how he was living it before, but what process has been able to take place in order to live it differently. As with "to be looked at", another subject may sum up the whole series of phenomena in his existence, as everything is done to make oneself looked at. It's not enough to acknowledge this moment, one also has to prove the change in the post-analysis relationship to the drive. Therefore, we have two dimensions at the end of an analysis: the advent of a new desire once crossed the level of the identifications, and a change at the level of the drive.

Here, it is appropriate to resume the distinction between the clinic of subject and the case-based clinic. The clinic of subject corresponds to the one contributing to identify the grammar of fantasy and of the drive. The case-based clinic enables detection of the singular manner to live the drive once one has identified its grammar, and the subject may then demonstrate how he moved beyond.

To move beyond fantasy already supposes reducing it to the singular. What's taken for granted is the notion of *fantasies* – in the plural – as activities of daytime reverie, already there in Freud when he evokes the hysterical reminiscences. When Freud says that hysterics suffer from reminiscences, it's to signal that the whole daytime reverie contributes to producing scenarios and being out of life. For Freud, the emphasis was on the past but it can also include scenarios about the future. The reveries are fantasies in the plural. If Lacan moves onto fantasy in the singular, it's because there is a structure of fantasy. In this sense, there is a crucial proposal in "The Subversion of the Subject and the Dialectic of Desire", where Lacan defines fantasy from effects of castration:

> Castration makes of phantasy a chain that is both supple and inextensible by which the fixation of object cathexis, which can hardly go

beyond certain natural limits, takes on the transcendental function of ensuring the jouissance of the Other that passes this chain on to me in the Law.[3]

What should be remembered as essential in this formulation, is the definition of fantasy as "a chain that is both supple and inextensible". The term *supple* indicates the variations of fantasy, the multiple. Indeed, for the same subject there are multiple formulations of fantasy, but at the same time, Lacan adds the term *inextensible* to indicate that there is a beginning and an end. "Inextensible", it's one limited thing – to which Lacan referred much earlier as a framework. In *The Anxiety*, Lacan makes use of the notion of framework in fantasy. When one poses fantasy as a chain, one establishes the link between fantasy and its limits because of a grammatical structure. Therefore, the chain Lacan refers to is the signifying chain. There is a signifying chain which ensures that fantasies may thrive, but they have a unique structure. It means that the course of an analysis consists of reducing this multiplicity of fantasies to a fundamental fantasy. Therefore, the idea of "inextensible" sends us back to the existence of a fundamental fantasy. Its specificity is the particular modality according to which a subject, from signifiers, has built up his subjective position. That's a thesis – I believe – which goes through the whole of Lacan's teaching, and Lacan sticks to it. That's why, with the traversal of fantasy, the analysts think they have found the ultimate form to what one may expect out of an analysis.

To return to this formulation in "The Subversion of the Subject and the Dialectic of Desire", Lacan adds that it can't override certain natural limits. It shows clearly that the subject finds his way through fantasy in his relationship to the Other's body, and that not everything is possible. There is an orientation, that of the subject from fantasy, but Lacan also says that's precisely the one which takes the role of ensuring the Other's *jouissance*, in other words, fantasy is in support of the subject's *jouissance*, but in a relationship to the Other's *jouissance*. There, the following phrase is interesting, since he says: "Anyone who really wants to come to terms with this Other has open to him the path of experiencing not the Other's demand, but its will". Then he goes on: "and then: to either realize himself as an object, turning himself into the mummy of some Buddhist initiation, or satisfy the will to castrate inscribed in the Other".[4] To satisfy the will to castrate inscribed in the Other, enables us to deduce that the neurotic's fantasy is: "The Other wants this from me, because it's its *jouissance*". It's assigning to the Other a will to *jouir* [rejoice], whose subject would be the object, would be "The Other wants *jouir de moi*" [rejoice in me]. For Lacan, there are two ways of seeing things: either one is making oneself the Other's object, or one comes to terms with the Other. According to this last option, Lacan makes use of a strong expression: "Anyone who really wants to come to terms with this Other". "To come to terms with" means to face, to feel, to experience. An experience of analysis means to come to terms with it, scene-by-scene, at close quarters as on a battle field, to finally conclude after a long course that the Other does not have the aim; we had imputed it. Therefore, the Other's want of castration, which the subject always believed in, does not exist. If the Other does not want my castration, then he does not want "*jouir de moi*" [*rejoice in me*]. It supposes two perspectives: on the one hand that of fantasy to bring alive this Other's *jouissance*, and on the other to traverse the identifications level. For those who made the choice to confront the Other, there is no other option than to pass through the ordeal of transference. It may adopt different forms and sometimes winding paths. It's sometimes what one may notice, when instead of confronting the fact that actually this Other does not exist, the subject does not give up to bring to life a substantial Other. We bring alive an Other which wants my *jouissance*. One may ask oneself the question: why does this widespread subjective position consist in bringing to life an Other which wants my castration?

The reason is given by Lacan in this same text: "The Subversion of the Subject and the Dialectic of Desire". The subject prefers above all that at least one escapes from castration, enabling him to have the illusion that he can also escape it. It's why the subject steps back from the idea to recognize the Other's lack.

The fantasy, in general, as Lacan says it in "Desire and its Interpretation", complies with a certain accommodation. This formulation is interesting, for it goes towards "a chain that is both supple and inextensible", as we've evoked. Thus, in his January 28th 1959 session, Lacan poses: "The phantasy satisfies a certain accommodation, a certain fixation of the subject, something which has an elective value".[5] It's that fantasy is not an opening to everything, it imposes exigencies, restrictions, it fixes the subject. The term of fixation, which harks back to the elective value that certain objects may have for the subject, is what will afterwards become "inextensible", regarding the signifying chain. These statements go towards what Freud evoked in terms of conditions of erotic infantile regarding the choice of sexual objects, and which decide the choices of partners during the adult life. That is to say that to get an erotic value, an object depends on fantasy. Of course, the Other's discourse is forged by the fantasy, it's why there exists some specific fantasies which are prevalent, and in our neo-liberal age, there are fantasies which seem similar for different subjects. That appears clearly, since for these subjects there is no significant difference between the articles of consumption goods. Indeed, how come, if we consider that everyone has one's fantasy, that the objects we desire are not so different from one subject to the other? That's a fact: there exists an impact of social discourse on the subject's fantasies. Where a difference emerges, it's in the formation of the fundamental fantasy and how each one forged his relationship with his "object *a*".

Here, another observation prevails about fantasy in psychosis. As we said, almost ten years after his formulation in "The Direction of the Treatment and the Principles of its Power", about the use of fantasy in the different clinical structures, Lacan asserts that during the opening-days on child psychosis: "the worth of psychoanalysis is that it operates on the fantasy".[6] Therefore, he gives us a direction to understand what the analytical clinic is, that is to say, to operate on fantasy; he adds: "its degree of success has demonstrated that there is judged the subjecting form, as neurosis, perversion or psychosis".[7] Why is he mentioning psychosis, while he talks about acting on fantasy? What do we mean by operating on fantasy in psychosis? Lacan focuses psychoanalysis, and even its efficacy, around effects on fantasy, but he mentions the three clinical structures. In other words, in my opinion, Lacan maintains not only the idea of fantasy in psychosis, but also of a possible effect. Personally, I certainly consider that the question of fantasy is excluded from schizophrenia, but remains relevant – as we incidentally mentioned with Freud – in paranoia. Then as we highlighted, just as he addresses in *From an Other to the other*, the inappropriate use of "choice" of the structure, in the "Address on Child Psychoses", Lacan resumes this conception to indicate "the misleading idea of a subjective 'choice' between neurosis, perversion and psychosis".[8] He focuses on "object *a*", as cause of desire in fantasy and he adds: "desire is, whereof fantasy is the *montage*".[9] If we accept that in psychosis it is a particular *montage* [montage], it is reasonable to assert that there exists a fantasy in certain forms of psychosis, and consequently, we can also argue for the existence of a desire in psychosis and accept the fact that there exists an incidence of analytical transference onto this desire.

The decision that matters

If we summon the term of *decision*, it's because it refers to something more than that of *choice*. One may have the idea that one has reached the end of one's analysis since one has retrieved the choice. It's a fact that if this choice was there since the beginning, we wouldn't have undergone an analysis. Therefore, the question of choice traverses all analyzes. Nevertheless, there is a time between the moment one retrieves the possibility to choose and the moment of the decision to conclude. Therefore, we can see clearly that with the question of the decision, we are at another level than that of the unconscious contradiction. A decision supposes that one does not revert. One decides something. It's strong a decision. It's a moment of conclusion. What's its basis? The decision to end an analysis rests on a certainty, certainty which is the answer given by the analysis to the initial indeterminacy. It's the result of the analytical operation.

Therefore, on one side we have the indeterminacy which keeps pace with the contradiction as a principle linked to the unconscious, and on the other side, the decision which keeps pace with certainty. It constitutes two poles, quite different. The contradiction is about truth from falsehood. As long as we are in search of what's true or what's false, basically we are still on the quest for another dimension which is that of truth, and there we find impasses since we always come across contradictions. That's something else to rest on certainty. First of all, it concerns the fact that I can cope with my symptom. To cope with one's symptom is what enabled Lacan to write it differently: *sinthome* [*le sinthome*]. We may postulate that the end of an analysis is the *certainty of sinthome* [*du sinthome*]. The *certainty of sinthome* [*du sinthome*], does not mean no symptom at all, it means to cope with the irreducibility of the symptom. It's why, at the end of an analysis course, it's not about producing one more "spoken word" [*un dit de plus*] but about overcoming the contradiction. That's also to acknowledge that it doesn't lead to another contradiction. To overcome the contradiction between "spoken words" [*les dits*] is extricating oneself from "spoken words" [*des dits*], as far as producing, as Lacan expressed it, "a viable atheist".

Once you succeed at reconsidering imaginary and symbolic, you realize that there is the production of a reduced identity to the fact that the body and the real are irrelevant. That's the meaning of the speaking-body [*le corps parlant*]. There is something of a body-speaking [*corps parlant*], even if it does not speak similarly as the hysteric's body. The speaking-body [*le corps parlant*] is a body which speaks but, unlike hysteria, it speaks meaninglessly. It is therefore indecipherable unless one talks nonsense about what it wants to say. But there is no proof that elucubration possesses a rational character. The speaking-body [*le corps parlant*] is an effect of the unconscious real, and it poses itself beyond the question of the unconscious knowledge. The unconscious real is a dimension which no longer falls under the supposition of knowledge. Therefore, the end of the analysis, from the moment we take into consideration the dimension of the real, is considering what's beyond the demand to the other. This idea of "beyond the supposition" is correlative to what Lacan defines as being the true formula of atheism: "God is unconscious".[10] To posit "God is unconscious", is to pose the idea of a supposition of knowledge. It's to indicate that somewhere it's known. That is God knows it. So that even for those who don't believe in God, they believe there will be a tomorrow. But how do we know it? When we live a day, we suppose that as it existed the day before, and exists the present day, there'll be a day after, but it's not a fact, it's a supposition. Therefore, it falls within the belief. One doesn't get rid easily of the dimension of belief, at least not like this!

The problem is: what's left when one gets rid of the belief? There is a risk for those who do not believe to be completely free. That's one of the definitions of schizophrenia. Schizophrenia is the absolute freedom. Besides, there is Lacan's formulation which must draw our attention: "Nothing is impossible for man, what he cannot he leaves. This is what is called mental health".[11] We realize the difference Lacan made between mental health and madness. Mental health is not of the order of "more constraints". It's mostly about the idea of having the choice. Madness, at the very least in its schizophrenic form, dwells in the absence of any constraint or choice, and what remains is the position which consists of refusing everything.

Therefore, it is appropriate to differentiate the one who is free from all constraint – the madman – from the one finding one's way through the impossibility. It would be the latter one who would be in the mental health. The absence of impossibility, which is another way to pose the absence of constraints, makes a reference to the absolute freedom. Absolute freedom is the position of a subject who can leave everything on an ongoing basis. That is precisely the paradox: someone claiming to be free, acting as a free creature, remains out of speech. In other words, what defines the schizophrenic, is that he does not consent to a discourse. That's interesting regarding the belief, since Lacan in his December 1973 and January 1974 seminars concerning "les non-dupes errent", mentions that the ones who are not deceived [*dupes*] will stand aimless. Therefore, for Lacan, to be deceived is a necessity for not erring. To be aimless is an effect of being out of speech, for not consenting to get into it, thus to refuse social links. He repeats what he put forward in terms of alienation and separation.

To enter into a discourse, alienation from the Other is required. Absolute freedom excludes all forms of alienation. In this sense, Lacan mentions the speaking-beings [*les êtres parlants*], saying that they have no other links than those of discourse. A speaking-being [*un être parlant*] defines himself through links of discourse. So, it's a condition of analysis to consent to a discourse, because to enter into the analytic discourse, one has to consent to it. It's a condition for the entry but not for its conclusion, because to consent to a discourse is a form of alienation, and with alienation one produces a false identity, an effect of the adequacy to the big Other [*au grand Autre*]. That's the difference between the alienated subject and the aimless one. The aimless subject is the one who does not consent to any form of alienation. The alienated subject creates a false identity, but he has the opportunity to step out. For as Lacan says, both principles of the "subject's causation"[12] are alienation and separation. Someone who's alienated from the Other may be able to part. On the contrary, there is no separation without previous alienation.

Let's note that Lacan, following his development about aimlessness, two years later returns to the Oedipus complex, and formulates: "everything is sustained in so far as the Name-of-the-Father is also the Father of the Name, which doesn't make the symptom any the less necessary".[13] In other words, the idea of the subject's structure requires the Name-of-the-Father [*le Nom-du-Père*], and the Name-of-the-Father [*le Nom-du-Père*] is out of the symbolic, enabling to name and therefore to knot imaginary and symbolic. For Lacan, the Name-of-the-Father [*le Nom-du-Père*], is coming in lieu of the Oedipus complex. In his last teaching, Lacan's move about the Oedipus is to introduce a new dimension that he poses as necessary. What is necessary is the symptom as the fourth element. To the imaginary, symbolic and real, he adds the symptom.

The symptom therefore, is the singular production which enables every subject to avoid aimlessness. Therefore, Lacan's idea is that for the subject it's not enough to be able to rely on the Name-of-the-Father [le Nom-du-Père]; in his last teaching, he poses that "for this name of the father, there is substituted a function which is none other than that of naming-to (nommer-à)".[14]. Then he specifies his proposition: "To be named to something is highlighted in an order which effectively being substituted for the Name of the Father".[15]

We may notice the transition from the Name-of-the-Father [le Nom-du-Père] and its function of introducing a particularity, which enables identification of the link between the symbolic and the imaginary in its relationship with the Other, to "naming-to (nommer-à)". With "naming-to (nommer-à)", we are at the core of the clinic of singularity, the one of case.

In the following seminar, Lacan resumes this axis with the term of exception when he poses:

> Anyone at all who reaches the function of exception that the father has, we know with what result, that of his Verwerfung, or of his rejection, in most cases, through the filiation that the father generates with the psychotic results that I have exposed.[16]

Here Lacan's reference is the father in his singular position, who escapes all discursive requirement. The father's exception opens up to a clinic conception focused onto what a case includes of exception regarding the others; that's the analytical experience's real dimension as being the one of a case-by-case basis.

I consider that it is in this direction that Lacan poses Joyce's case: "It is clear, however, that Joyce's art is something so particular that the term sinthome is really what suits it".[17] Indeed, when one expresses that it is "so particular", it's because one considers that it is the exception relating to a singularity. In this sense, it constitutes a model. In psychoanalysis, the case-based clinic would aim to grasp each case as being "so particular".

Psychoanalysis, science, and religion

This is what brings us back to the unconscious. The hypothesis of unconscious supposes that from the outset exists a supposition on the analyst's behalf, that there'll be some unconscious to be found in a subject. Indeed, to pose the unconscious in terms of hypothesis is actually what Freud set out to do. Here, significantly, Lacan resumes Freud. Therefore, it must be said that, when he asks the question of the hypothesis of the unconscious, it's not in terms of a religious belief, it's not a dogma.

However, there is an aspect in psychoanalysis which may suggest it. Lacan himself perceived the risks when he discusses the Freudian conception of the psychical reality. Thus, he formulates:

> With his Name-of-the-Father, which is identical to psychical reality, to what he calls psychical reality, specifically to religious reality, for it is exactly the same thing, that it is thus by this function, by this function of the dream that Freud establishes the link of the Symbolic, the Imaginary and the real.[18]

Therefore, Lacan is far from the idea of making use of the Name-of-the-Father [*le Nom-du-Père*] as a tool to bring a religious dogma to psychoanalysis. That's moreover the reason why, regarding this question, he distances himself from Freud and also why he pluralizes the Name-of-the-Father [*le Nom-du-Père*] to the Names-of-the-Father [*les Noms-du-Père*]. The essential then, becomes what for each one works as an exception.

To pose the unconscious as a hypothesis is in line with the scientific conception. For example, we keep on saying "theory of relativity" in physics; we don't say "law of relativity". A theory, even if it has been admitted, leaves open the possibility to be disproved, while with a law, we are sure each time of our ability to demonstrate it and that nothing may be objected. To pose the idea of a theory, such as that of relativity, or the idea of the hypothesis of the unconscious, is to accept that someday it may be denied. Therefore, when one says "theory" or when one says "hypothesis", it's a question of method. It's the starting point of every experience of analysis. From the idea of a supposition, one could believe that's something in common with religion. Nevertheless, the difference with religion is that the hypothesis of the unconscious has to be proved for each analysis. In this sense, it's not a dogma. So, what is Lacan's idea about belief and what does it become after an analysis?

The idea of belief, is not only the idea of the hypothesis. There is a substrate to belief. That's clearly expressed in *The Four Fundamental Concepts of Psychoanalysis* with the signifying dialectic. What is founding the belief, is the bond between a signifier and an-other [*un autre*]. And, on the contrary, when signifiers don't work that way, but as a unique body, there we are in the disruption of the articulation, which Lacan illustrates from a series of phenomena linked to unbelief. The *unbelief* [*l'incroyance*], is one of the first terms Freud had found to evoke psychosis. What is founding the belief, is the idea of an interval, an opening, a pending second signifier which must happen.

Now, when we say the hypothesis of the unconscious, it's because, on the analyst's side, we suppose that in an analysis we'll have some effects onto the unconscious. We can promise nothing but we suppose that because of the analysis, a subject will be differently affected by his unconscious. That is justifying the notion of the analyst's "act". If the analyst produces an act, it's because he supposes that he'll be able to affect the subject's unconscious.

With this notion of act, we possess what in Lacan's theory and practice, substitutes for the absence of guarantee in the symbolic. Lacan, for a very long time, believed in the idea of a symbolic which could be complete. Besides, his first formulations of the Name-of-the-Father [*le Nom-du-Père*], were to pose the Name-of-the-Father [*le Nom-du-Père*] as the Other to the Other. What would ensure the whole? It would be a signifier founding the whole and therefore able to give a foundation to the law. Therefore, it's a signifier having a substitute function. It poses the Name-of-the-Father [*le Nom-du-Père*] as an exception. Lacan has already the idea that there must be a plus [*un plus*], that something must work for a subject to ensure this plus [*ce plus*] which brings a support for the whole. Therefore, that is precisely the idea of the Name-of-the-Father [*le Nom-du-Père*] as the Other being a guarantor. That's the function Freud assigned to the father, then by extension to God. Therefore, we see that at that time Lacan believed that the structure was dependent on the symbolic. Yet, after *Anxiety*, a shift was coming, when Lacan lectured the unique lesson "The Names-of-the-Father" [*les Noms-du-Père*]. He will not pursue this lesson, but the idea to pluralize this signifier, and to pose The Names-of-the-Father [*les Noms-du-Père*] gives already the idea that it is not about a unique signifier as embodying the exception but that there exists a plural. It's explicit in the formulation "...the Name of the Father. Which means nothing at the start, not simply the father as name, but the father as naming".[19] It's because of the father as the one who's naming, that the exception supports itself.

In the last part of *The Four Fundamental Concepts of Psychoanalysis*, as Freud had already done, Lacan resumes the links between psychoanalysis, religion, and science. It's a question to which Lacan returns throughout his teaching. I single out the analyst's relationship to fraud. What proves that claiming to be an analyst is not an assertion of fraud? Regarding the psychoanalyst, what in a way ensures it is the guarantee given by the others. In Freud's times, it was Freud who was giving his guarantee. To authorize oneself, according to Lacan's proposition, implies that the analysand's analyst can't be the guarantor that there is no fraud. So, when one authorizes oneself, does one do it through one's fantasy, that is to say the will to be an analyst, or does one do it because the desire to be analyst came during the treatment? It would be the only guarantee that there is no fraud.

This part of *The Four Fundamental Concepts of Psychoanalysis* marks specifically the psychoanalysis status as being different from the religious one and distinct from science. It's different from religion in that psychoanalysis deals with the lack in the Other, that lack being sutured in all religions. The principle of religion is to pose the status of a complete Other; psychoanalysis instead has a method and practical orientation to pose as a starting principle that there exists some lack in the Other. Psychoanalysis takes care of desire, but to take care of desire and to take care of lack in the Other, it's exactly the same thing. Why is that? Because for a subject there is no desire if he hasn't experienced the lack in the Other. That is also crucial for the direction of the treatment – as we already said – it's essential that the subject may be confronted by the fact that the Other is lacking [*manquant*]. And we may measure the effects: the more the subject experiences the lack in the Other, the more for the subject a dimension of dismay is taking place, of disorientation, which at the same time is a necessary condition to move toward a desire.

Science aims towards harmony; that is, to get rid of discontinuities. That's why Lacan was able to demonstrate that the adventures of History, linked – in antique histories – to the existence of empires, are the same as science's aim. That is to say that history, with its empires, aims to reduce the discontinuities, to produce a continuum meant to ensure an authority from knowledge. Indeed, it's about producing a knowledge where some flaws could appear. Psychoanalysis instead supports the idea of a disjunction, of a discontinuity, which is one of the names used to designate the flaw in a subject. That's also the disjunction between knowledge and authority. That illustrates precisely what science wishes, namely to constitute an apparatus of knowledge to run a complete knowledge. Thus, what's aimed at is the production of a universal law of the norm. That is precisely the idea of universality of science. It enables us to think about our current science, how it operates, how it works, and the little space it leaves to the subject. That's what led Lacan to speak about the subject's foreclosure due to science. Lacan says explicitly "the field of this no doubt successful science, which ours is in so far as in the whole of its physical field it has succeeded in foreclosing the subject".[20] Then in 1970, he repeats the proposition: "science is an ideology of the suppression of the subject".[21] Psychoanalysis doesn't make use of knowledge as an authority, but rather makes use of the inadequacies of knowledge. Lacan's search lies at the level of what is missing in Freud's elaboration and it's precisely what invites us to pursue. The analytical approach does not aim to carry on from learned knowledge [*savoir acquis*], but rather track the flaws of knowledge. That's why Lacan emphasizes "object *a*".

"Object *a*" dramatically incarnates the rest: what remains of the operation between the subject and the Other. It incarnates the dimension of flaw in the Other. It's from this perspective that must be seized the question of transference and his future at the end of analysis. There is a criticism formulated very early on by Lacan about the term of "liquidation of transference". Our transference regarding psychoanalysis doesn't stop by the end of the treatment. If the term is inappropriate, it's because there is something which liquidates itself by the end of an analysis and something which doesn't. One doesn't liquidate transference as a whole. What one liquidates, is the deception of love. If an analysis should enable the subject to learn something, it's how there exists a dimension of deception in love. Love in transference is deceptive because it leads towards a closure of the unconscious. In analysis, it's striking for a number of subjects: it's not exceptional to not only experience love in transference, but to feel the certainty that the analyst and nobody else is the object of this love in transference. For them, the object of love, they have met it and it's not only a substitution. Sometimes it causes problems for the remainder of the analysis, since why continue free association if one has already found love? This is also verified in psychosis. The erotomania of transference in psychosis, which occasionally may take a platonic form, may become an exigency of *jouissance*, since the subject is convinced that the partner is this one and no one else. Therefore, when one says that one liquidates the deception of love, what one liquidates is the symptomatic seduction performed by the subject in order to be seen as a loveable object.

Lacan used to say that love is mutual. It does not mean that each time one is in love, one may be sure to be loved by one's partner. Mutual love means that if one is in love, it's because one seeks to be a loveable object, and that's precisely the transference problematic, since transference is necessary for the course of the treatment, but it's also a hindrance if it settles onto the idea that the subject wants to be loveable to the other. That is precisely the analysand's seduction, seduction which must be brought to a conclusion, that is to say, gotten to the end of. In other words, love in transference is at the service of the ideal of the self, that's what the subject is aiming at, to see himself as seen by the other. If the other sees me as loveable, I tell myself that I am loveable. Therefrom, Lacan will demonstrate the necessary distance to be produced in analysis between idealization and "object *a*". That's the necessary gap which must be produced during the treatment. For this reason, Lacan is making use of the term of "maneuver of transference", which he also mentions for psychosis to indicate the adjustment which must take place between the point where the subject sees himself as loveable, and the point where the subject is caused by the lack. It is this point of lack that the subject has to recognize and about which he has to recognize himself.

Psychoanalysis therefore establishes itself as the reverse of religion and keeps its distance with science. At the center of religion and science there exists the idea of the complete Other; yet not only the psychoanalysis starting point is the Other's incompleteness, but more fundamentally, this incompleteness, psychoanalysis radicalizes. The effects of analysis onto the religious belief should be examined. What must be noticed, is that *From an Other to the other*, Lacan refers to atheism exactly as he had evoked it in *The Four Fundamental Concepts of Psychoanalysis* where he posed, as we have said, that "God is unconscious". In *From an Other to the other*, he provides a formulation for atheism, which he'll later resume in his conferences in the United States. He formulates that "True atheism – the only atheism that deserves the name – is the atheism that results from calling the subject-supposed-to-know [*le sujet-supposé-savoir*] into question".[22] Here Lacan, from his conception about transference and its future, discusses the relationship to religion. Indeed, the subject-supposed-to-know [*le sujet-supposé-savoir*] idea is based on a belief in the Other. We notice an astonishing connection between psychoanalysis and religion. There is in psychoanalysis, a requirement of belief in the subject-supposed-to-know [*le sujet-supposé-savoir*], and the Other is supposed to be the location of knowledge. Lacan's thesis is that the subject-supposed-to-know [*le sujet-supposé-savoir*] model, is the same as the God of the philosophers, and it's why he affirms: "the subject supposed-to-know is God" and he adds: "that's the end of the story".[23]

So, the idea is that religion is an Other in which one believes, deeply, whole-heartedly, without any possible questioning. It's similar for the subject-supposed-to-know [*le sujet-supposé-savoir*] but nevertheless with a difference. For religion, this Other is a big Other wholly consistent and there appears the necessity to evoke the lack in the Other. So that there is in analysis the constitution of a subject-supposed-to-know [*le sujet-supposé-savoir*], the subject must have a glimpse of the Other's inconsistence. The supposed knowledge is a supposition which deals with the lack of knowledge on the subject's side. That's why Lacan says that the analysts must be up to date with the discourse they handle, the analytic discourse. What is specific to the religious, to the religion and to the religious use, is that in religion, one leaves the responsibility of the cause to the Other. While what founds somebody's position as analysand, is that he must assume responsibility of the cause. In this sense, we understand why, if the subject-supposed-to-know [*le sujet-supposé-savoir*] has something to do with religion, he is also in conflict with it. In the transference's ordeal, the analyst must lead the subject to face the non-existence of the subject-supposed-to-know [*le sujet-supposé-savoir*], and the flaw in the Other. It's the reason why Lacan adds that "It is not clear that it is possible for thought to face this question, or even formulating it constitutes any sort of step in this direction".[24] In other words, it's a difficult question to confront, that of the non-existence of a complete Other. Therefore, when Lacan says that's it's impossible for thought to confront it, he means that it has to be confronted by transference, through ordeal, and said differently, through affects. This is something in analysis that the analyst must make the subject feel.

Therefore, naturally the question arises: what does the belief become at the end of analysis, once the subject has been able to identify his own share, his responsibility, what he didn't want to know, that is to say the share of *jouissance*, that he henceforth knows falls upon him? That's what Lacan will resume in a later text, where he discusses the effects of analysis upon belief. We'll get to it.

But before that should be evoked the link between religion and clinical structures, which again demonstrates the necessity to move beyond the structures-based clinic and to focus the microscope onto the singularity.

Indeed, Lacan mentions:

Thus, subjects of one type are of no use to others of the same type. And it is even conceivable that an obsessional not be able to make the least sense of the discourse of another obsessional. This is even how religious wars get started, if it is true that for religion (for this is the only trait that makes them a class, moreover insufficient), obsession is in the mix.[25]

Here, the idea which is put forward is not new. To share the same structure includes no privilege as to understanding who is the other. There are no special affinities between the subjects of the same structure. And Lacan's example is that of the obsessional. Lacan adds nothing new. He had already posed that obsessive neurosis is an intra-subjective structure. That is to say, that it demonstrates it is the subject's debate with himself, without any possibility, as is the case in hysteria, to deliver a discourse which would be specific to the structure. Therefore, there is a hysteric discourse but not an obsessional one.

Of course, there is a religious discourse but it remains insufficient to access the other status of discourses. And if Lacan mentions the war between religions, it's from Freud's idea about obsession as a private religion. In this sense, there exists a convergence between the obsessional, the religion, and the war. As early as 1907, in his article "Obsessive Acts and Religious Practices", Freud proceeded towards a convergence between religious rites and private rites of obsessive neurosis. If we admit that rites aim to protect from anxiety, the same function should be assigned to religious rites. Lacan himself in the *Ethics* poses the affinity between religion and obsessive neurosis. And even regarding war, he had already mentioned the obsessional as an inexpungable fortress. War between religions conjoins the three dimensions already mentioned: the destruction of the other's desire, the intra-subjective withdrawal, and the necessity to uphold one's existence with those whom we believe share the same belief.

Therefore, when Lacan poses that obsessional neurosis makes use of religion to look classy [*faire classe*], and that it remains insufficient, it's because this process of sharing, that of religious community, can't be elevated to the category of discourse. There is certainly a religious discourse, but it remains insufficient to accede to the other status of discourses.

The "viable atheist"

In the "Conferences and Conversations at North American Universities", Lacan poses – simultaneously as a question and as an assertion – is psychoanalysis able to make a "viable atheist"? Therefore, here it's not the "true atheist" mentioned in *From an Other to the other*, but a "viable atheist". He defines it: "It's someone who does not contradict oneself all the time".[26] It seems simple, "someone who does not contradict oneself all the time"! I think that what it is about, in this assertion from Lacan, is the decision to conclude the analysis and afterwards the relationship to the unconscious.

The decision to conclude is in some way to say goodbye to the unconscious, at least to the demand of deciphering. That does not mean that we are parting from the unconscious; the unconscious remains the subject's Other, but the subject is no longer traversed by the unconscious contradictions. It is a major change to be expected from an analysis. Freud posed as a principle of the functioning of the unconscious, the fact that it does not know the contradictions. What is the analytical translation to these contradictions? Let's take this well-known example. During the first weekly session, the subject says "A"; at the second session, three days later, and without any difficulty, he says "B", in strict opposition to what he had said with his phrase "A". Therefore, he substitutes a statement for another one based on a different assertion from the former, and without causing the slightest worry, so much so that one wonders how it is that the analysand may affirm such opposite statements in so short a time. Thus, the subject may state without embarrassment, one thing and its opposite. All these contradictions constitute the clue that we are determined by unconscious signifiers. The unconscious yields signs to the subject through formations of the unconscious. These formations do not allow conclusions, and make of the subject someone inevitably undetermined by the unconscious, by the contradictions. The unconscious doesn't know that contradiction means the unconscious may display one thing and its opposite. The consequences for the subject are that he is unable to conclude with his unconscious, since perforce the unconscious displays conflicting signs. Indeed, how rely on his unconscious if sometimes the signs displayed are divergent with one another? Therefore, there must be another operation to be able to end the indetermination in which the subject is immersed because of the unconscious.

The God hypothesis is something else; it's on the analyst's side. It implies to assume, in the analysand, an irreducible place where the saying [le dire] could be produced. Lacan shifted from the formulation God to Dieur [God = Dieu in French + r] and then to the saying [Dieu then Dieur then dire]. It means that the analyst assumes a saying [un dire]. To assume a saying [un dire] means that beyond a patient's "spoken words" [dits], there is his saying [son dire]. Furthermore, it's the reason why Lacan posed that theologians are those who speak about God and in doing so are the atheists. It's paradoxical; to talk about God is the condition of atheism, but also, as everybody knows, when one speaks about something, one brings it into existence. Speaking about it, one makes subsisting something of the Other. It's the same thing for the unconscious, in analysis it's while speaking about a thing, and from the analysand's "spoken words" [les dits] that a saying [un dire] is possible. At the same time, it is by speaking about it that one reduces God's place. The more we confront someone to one's contradictions, the more it is possible to seize what determines them. That's precisely in analysis what we are aiming at.

In Lacan, there is the idea that the Other is no longer at the end of an analysis. If the Other is no more, the idea of belief is impossible, neither in a God nor in a substitute who would come instead. At the same time, certainly there is something which remains from the Other's dimension. Therefore, to what extent does it change radically the Other's existence? It's very difficult to formulate, and clearly it is different depending on whether the subject was a true believer or not before the onset of the analysis. For example, it's not identical for people who were in religious orders, and then became analysts. Well known people spoke about their experience, and one asked them the question, "After the analysis, do you no longer believe in God?" Thus, we have the example of an analyst having left the orders and, regarding that question, for some time stayed silent, then answered: "it's difficult to answer." It's why Lacan concludes with the proposition of a viable atheist. That's not a radical atheist, nor the absolute unbeliever, it is viable, at each time, for each one, a point which has to be touched on. To what extent? Certainly there exist variations according to the starting point in the experience.

The question is about knowing if God is a symptom, and if it has to be dealt with. God is a symptom, I guess that would be the formulation of theology. There are those who deal with the question of God, and therefore it's a symptom. Is God a symptom for all? For sure, if someone at the beginning is radically a believer, as soon as he starts questioning it, it becomes a symptom. In this case and with this God-symptom there is a know-how, but we can't say that it is a symptom for all.

Yet, the "viable atheist" is a way to take a stand regarding the belief in the unconscious. Once one has confronted the question of the belief in the unconscious, there is a moment when the switch happens and in which lies the fact of ceasing to be on the lookout for the slightest sign of one's own unconscious. This distance regarding one's own unconscious, is at some point the reason why one doesn't feel the need to tell an analyst something about oneself. At the same time, it is what prepares one to receive the other's unconscious, for those who decide to become analysts. When one reaches this moment in transference, it doesn't mean that one doesn't believe in the unconscious, it's rather that one doesn't feel anymore the necessity to address a message to the Other. One makes oneself responsible for the unconscious' "spoken words" [dits]. On the other hand, it is more interesting to decipher the other's unconscious. Therefore, the contradiction is of the order of true or false. The "true atheist" is the one who doesn't try to cope with true or false. It's the one who knows how to cope with one's symptom.[27]

To cope with one's symptom is something other than the contradiction. As long as we are in contradictions, we are in the quest of one more "spoken word" [dit]: we try one more "spoken word" [dit] hoping that the following one will be the true one. To overcome the contradiction is to extricate one-self from the "spoken words" [les dits]. Here one can correlate the "viable atheist" with the real unconscious. One measures the real unconscious from what remains of the symptom at the end of the analysis. It's not that the real unconscious shows up and makes a sign at the end of the analysis! It becomes the subject's partner at the end of the analysis. It's what the subject will have to cope with, no more with his contradictions, but with this reduced identity which is about a real out-of-meaning [*hors sens*] which is the crucial modality of the relationship between the body and the real. To be confronted like this, it gives an irreducible point of identity to any change. From this moment one may do without unconscious knowledge. Logically, it leads to the end of the analysis.

Let's discuss this moment concerning the decision of passage to the analyst [*passage à l'analyste*]. When Lacan says "he is only authorized by himself [...] and by some others", wherefrom does one authorize oneself?[28] And who are these others? Does it refer to Freud and Lacan or does it refer to a school?

I believe that the answer is clear. Lacan's idea is that to authorize oneself is only from an act. The act is an act done by a subject. Therefore, it can't come from the Other. It's against the idea which was existing at that time, whereby it's the analyst who says if one has reached the end. Therefore, inevitably the conclusion stems from a subject's act. But by promoting at the same time the idea of "from some others", for Lacan it means that concomitantly and inseparably, this act has to be demonstrated to an analytic community. If the act supposes to do without the Other, it's not however to get rid of the Other. Obviously, when Lacan proposes it, there is the necessity of an analytic community. It's this community which becomes the Other for the subject regarding psychoanalysis. A community which is not without Freud's texts, Lacan's, and some others.

From symptom to *sinthome*

The theoretical change aims to understand that the real unconscious is inseparable from Lacan's shift consisting of a switch from the Name-of-the-Father [*le Nom-du-Père*] to the father as a naming function, to which the symptom must be joined as necessary. Therefore, here there is a change, we go from the Name-of-the-Father [*le Nom-du-Père*] as a guarantee, to the necessity of something having a naming function. The Name-of-the-Father [*le Nom-du-Père*] is required but it doesn't make the symptom less necessary.

This shift is the consequence for having perceived the limits of the significance of symbolic, and these limits appeared distinctly as to the impossibility of dispelling the symptom opacity. In other words, in the symptom, there is something which doesn't let itself be elucidated by the symbolic, therefore by the interpretation. Of course, the symptom may be deciphered. Nevertheless, it remains irreducible concerning its *jouissance*. There is a part of *jouissance* which doesn't let itself be captured by the analytic apparatus.

That's why in a coherent manner, one understands why Lacan provides as a definition of the real, the real *ex-sistence*, in other words out of reach of the symbolic. It exists, but it exists outside, it means in a place apart from the symbolic one.

Therefore, Lacan advanced the idea that to suppose the Name-of-the-Father [*le Nom-du-Père*], is to make it an equal of God.

> The hypothesis of the unconscious, and Freud underscores this, is something that can only hold up by presupposing the Name-of-the-Father. Presupposing the Name-of-the-Father, which is certainly God, is how psychoanalysis, when it succeeds, proves that the Name-of-the-Father can just as well be bypassed [...] on the condition that one make use of it.[29]

We'll come further to what may be understood by the success of a psychoanalysis. But before one may ask oneself: who is supposing? The analyst supposes that the Name-of-the-Father [*le Nom-du-Père*] is on the analysand's side. It's claimed in *Encore* when Lacan says that the subject is the subject of the unconscious. Therefore, when we say, the hypothesis of the unconscious, it means at the same time supposing that there is a subject. Thus, the idea is that the subject is not at the start of the analysis; the subject must be produced.

Therefore, the hypothesis of the unconscious is the idea that this unconscious may become the subject's Other. In the everyday life, does a subject who is not in analysis, when he makes a slip of the tongue, accept the responsibility of this slip? He may sometimes say that it is a slip, he admits it, but he never tries to analyze the reason why he made it. Therefore, he does not take a responsibility for this slip. At most, he interprets it in the light of his fantasy.

Therefore, to say that the unconscious becomes the subject's Other, is rather supporting the necessity of an operation, that of the analysis, to bring into existence the unconscious, and then that which a subject is responsible for. There would be a counterexample to the idea of supposition, it would be the scientific discourse.

The scientific discourse doesn't sustain itself with the idea of supposition, since it starts from a premise which is that of the utmost integral transmission of a knowledge. Therefore, it must be possible to demonstrate everything. Refutation is not possible, otherwise one rules out the idea of hypothesis. If one rules out the hypothesis, one is in complete transmission. Here, one sees an affinity between science and what Lacan with Freud called, the successful paranoia. The successful paranoia is the suture of all possible flaws. The problem is that it produces a total closure; no dialectics between signifiers, it's rather the fixity, or as Lacan says it in one of his latest definitions of paranoia, it's the frozen desire.

I revert to the *sinthome*. It must be considered from an idea, which for Lacan is a constant idea, already posed in *The Formations of the Unconscious*, when he says "The Name-of-the-Father, but it is also necessary to know how to use it".[30] In other words, he has the idea – right at the moment he poses the idea of The Name-of-the-Father [*le Nom-du-Père*] as an exception which ensures the whole – that to dispose of this signifier Name-of-the-Father [*le Nom-du-Père*] is not an insurance either, for you have to know how to use it. It gives us the idea that in a number of phenomena in which the subject disposes of The Name-of-the-Father [*le Nom-du-Père*], he doesn't know how to use it, for example anxiety.

Anxiety is failing to mobilize a signifier when one is confronted to the enigma of the Other's desire, and that besides, one is concerned. That's the encounter with a hole, but it's not the hole of a lack of signifier, but rather the hole of the inability to mobilize it. Therefore, it already gives the idea Lacan was having in 1958, that to possess the signifier Name-of-the-Father [*le Nom-du-Père*] is insufficient, you still need to be able to mobilize it.

That's also true for the inhibition. Inhibition exemplifies the case where one disposes of the signifier Name-of-the-Father [*le Nom-du-Père*], nevertheless the subject must find an additional solution to sustain himself in the existence, which is to introduce limits at the imaginary level. Then, beside inhibition and anxiety, there is the symptom. Amongst the definitions given by Freud, there is one that should here be recalled: the symptom as "compensation". It indicates that for the subject, there exists a default of satisfaction, and that he has to find it elsewhere. I find that this formulation coming from Freud makes obsolete all post-Freudian analytical considerations about notion of reparation. For there is already in the structure an internal repairer, it's the symptom. The symptom compensates, in other words, it takes responsibility for the satisfaction the subject doesn't find elsewhere.

So, out of the idea that you still have to know how to use The Name-of-the-Father [*le Nom-du-Père*], we return to the latest notion from Lacan, the notion of substitute. The substitute is an artifice in the subject's structure in order to make it stick together, in the absence of symptom. That's the idea that in *The Sinthome* Lacan draws out about Joyce. The substitute comes instead of symptom.

The step – I don't find it absurd – is to consider the term of *sinthome* that Lacan reserves for Joyce, and to expand and to pose it for the whole of the clinic. I think that it is deduced from Lacan's teaching, even if through his demonstration it can't be completely certain. It is deduced from Joyce and his constant need for writing, which poses a substitute. The substitute is something which is of the order of: "one doesn't cease to have to use it". In other words, there is an eternal renewal of the writing dimension, and from this artifice to sustain himself towards what he's missing. In *The Sinthome*, about Joyce, Lacan mentions his start in life. He says: "one couldn't get off to a worse start than he did",[31] which brings us back to the question of the subject's choice. It gives the idea that for a subject there are specific conjunctions which determine his destiny. Therefore, "one couldn't get off to a worse start than he did", means that the situation when he was born didn't make it easy for him. It also means that he started with a handicap, that he had no choice about the starting point, all this to highlight the fact that one doesn't have all the choice.

Nevertheless, what is important to understand is Lacan's change of perspective. He often mentioned as a fact far from rare, that one may have a poor start in the existence. That is to say, what does it mean to have a poor start in the existence? It's to be undesired. That is a constant in Lacan, as soon as he posed that "the subject bears the mark of the Other's desire". If the subject hasn't been desired, there is no mark. And therefore, in connection with the fact of being undesired, he has mentioned the idea of a necessary compensation on the subject's side facing the Other's absence of desire. Therefore, when we speak about the necessary compensation, we are in the register of choice, and precisely there, we are in the register of the subject's choice of *jouissance*. Therefore, the subject's choice is the *jouissance* compensation with regard to what was missing at the start.

Therefore, when one says that Joyce is off to a bad start, this time, it's not about the desire of the Other maternal. We notice few remarks in Joyce about the mother's desire, and it's not Lacan's focus. Nor is it the biographers' focus who rarely make any reference to it. Besides, he very rarely mentions it. Therefore, to be off to a bad start regarding him, in my opinion, is linked to what Lacan called "the de facto foreclosure". The de facto foreclosure is about the position of paternal dismissal even before Joyce was born. That's very clear in the seminar. In front of the father's dismissal, it was necessary for a substitute to occur. Therefore, this one is the subject's answer. The answer was a continuous operation onto the writing of language. Therefore, this is an invention which requires an "understand how to take advantage". It demonstrates how to do without the father is something else than going further than the father. To go further than the father, is a formulation which is appropriate to neurosis. Freud, unable to go the Acropolis, gives the reasons of his inhibition. It's the difficulty to go further than his father. Here, it's something else, it's doing without the paternal dismissal. Yet again, one measures the efficiency of his invention to the fact that he also did without God.

I will resume another formulation, which in my opinion converges with that of being a heretic in the already mentioned proper way, which is: "Presupposing the Name-of-the-Father, which is certainly God, is how psychoanalysis, when it succeeds, proves that the Name-of-the-Father can just as well be bypassed. One can just as bypass it, on the condition that one make use of it".[32]

The "make use of it" puts us in the perspective of what afterwards Lacan elaborated with the term of *substitute*. Joyce in *The Sinthome* is the example. So, why relate the question of substitute and "make use of it"? Joyce demonstrates the idea of the substitute by the fact that it's about an artifice which is not once and for all, but that it takes a necessary character. It's necessary in the sense of a constant use. In his case, the constant use is that of a writing practice. The substitute complies with a "it doesn't cease to be in progress". Joyce doesn't cease to have to use the writing practice.

Therefore, I return to the father question; in neurosis, it's to do without fantasy, without nostalgia of the father. In Freud, there is the idea of believing in the father, as founder of the subject's belief. The idea "to do without", doesn't mean ceasing to believe, but to believe in the proper way; so, to be heretic in the proper way, it's knowing how to make use of one's symptom. This know-how on a man's side towards a woman, it's not the same as to believe her. On the woman's side, it's not only about ceasing to believe in the man, but it's also being able to do without the Other woman and make use of the unconscious to incarnate one.

I resume by other means the former question, namely in an analysis, when does one get rid of the father? According to Lacan, God exists in the structure. Hence, he formulates "that the symbolic is the support of what became God, is beyond doubt".[33] Then he says it explicitly: "in short, he is *repression in person*, he is even *the person presupposed for repression*. And it is in that *that it is true*".[34]

That is to say, that as soon as one supposes something, it's because one doesn't know, but that somewhere, it could be known. Here, there is a cutting of the existence of a function, and it's there precisely that stays God's function. Therein religion has something real. Actually, if God was existing, it would be the Other's Other. Lacan's idea is to put in its place what he calls the true hole. The hole, that is to say that there is no Other's Other.

It's in this theoretical context that it is appropriate to highlight that in psychoanalysis the clinic of case supposes that one finds, at the end of an analysis, in the absolute difference linked to the name of the symptom, the necessary consistency enabling confrontation of what may arise in life as an enigma, but also what appears as an unpredictable real.

Notes

1 Lacan, J., *Le Séminaire, Livre XXIV, l'Insu que sait de l'une-bévue s'aile à mourre*, leçon du 16 novembre 1976. (*Seminar XXIV: Final Sessions.* Wednesday 16 November 1976, p. 3. Translation by C. Gallagher.)
2 Lacan, J. Séminaire XXIV "La direction de la cure et les principes de son pouvoir", *Écrits*. Paris, Le Seuil, 1976, pp. 585–645. (*Direction of the Treatment and the Principles of Its Power*. New York and London, W.W Norton & Company. Translated by B. Fink in collaboration with H. Fink and R. Grigg.
3 Lacan, J., « Subversion du sujet et dialectique du désir dans l'inconscient freudien » In *Écrits*, Paris, Le Seuil, 1966, p. 826. ("The Subversion of the Subject and the

Dialectic of Desire in the Freudian Unconscious", *Écrits*, New York and London, W.W. Norton and Company, 2002, p. 700. Translation by B. Fink in collaboration with H. Fink.)

4   Lacan, J., « Subversion du sujet et dialectique du désir dans l'inconscient freudien », in *Écrits*, Paris, Le Seuil, 1966, p. 826. ("The Subversion of the Subject and the Dialectic of Desire in the Freudian Unconscious", *Écrits*, New York and London, W.W. Norton and Company, 2002, p. 700. Translation by B. Fink in collaboration with H. Fink.)

5   Lacan, J., Séminaire VI "Le désir et son interpretation", Paris, La Martinière, 2013. (*The Seminar of Jacques Lacan Book VI: Desire and its Interpretation*, p. 151. Translated by C. Gallagher.)

6   Lacan, J, « Allocution sur les psychoses de l'enfant », in *Autres écrits*, Paris, le Seuil, 2001, p. 366. ("Address on Child Psychoses", p. 273. Translation by A. Price & B. Khiara-Foxton.)

7   Lacan, J, « Allocution sur les psychoses de l'enfant », in *Autres écrits*, Paris, le Seuil, 2001, p. 366. ("Address on Child Psychoses", p. 273. Translation by A. Price & B. Khiara-Foxton.)

8   Lacan, J, « Allocution sur les psychoses de l'enfant », in *Autres écrits*, Paris, le Seuil, 2001, p. 367. ("Address on Child Psychoses", p. 274. Translation by A. Price & B. Khiara-Foxton.)

9   Lacan, J, « Allocution sur les psychoses de l'enfant », in *Autres écrits*, Paris, le Seuil, 2001, p. 368. ("Address on Child Psychoses", p. 275. Translation by A. Price & B. Khiara-Foxton.)

10 Lacan, J., *Le Séminaire, Livre XI, Les quatre concepts fondamentaux de la psychanalyse*, p. 58. (*The Four Fundamental Concepts of Psychoanalysis, From Interpretation to the Transference: The Seminar of Jacques Lacan, Book XI*, W.W. Norton and Company, New York and London, p. 53. Translation by A. Sheridan.)

11 Lacan, J., *Le Séminaire, Livre XXI, Les non-dupes errant*, leçon du 15 janvier 1974. (*The Seminar of Jacques Lacan Book XXI Les non-dupes errent*. Seminar 6: Tuesday 15 January 1974, p. 122. Translation by C. Gallagher.)

12 Lacan, J., « Position de l'inconscient » In *Écrits*, Paris, Le Seuil, 1966, pp. 839–840. ("Position of the Unconscious", *Écrits*, New York and London, W.W. Norton and Company, 2002, p. 712. Translation by B. Fink in collaboration with H. Fink.)

13 Lacan, J., *Le Séminaire, Livre XXIII, Le sinthome* p. 22. (*The Sinthome: The Seminar of Jacques Lacan, Book XXIII*. Polity Press, Cambridge, 2018, p. 13. Translation by A.R. Price.)

14 Lacan, J., *Le Séminaire, Livre XXI, Les non-dupes errent*, leçon du 20 mars 1974. (*The Seminar of Jacques Lacan Book XXI Les non-dupes errent*, Seminar 10, p. 183. Translation by C. Gallagher.)

15 Lacan, J., *Le Séminaire, Livre XXI, Les non-dupes errent*, leçon du 20 mars 1974. (*The Seminar of Jacques Lacan Book XXI Les non-dupes errent*, Seminar 10, p. 184. Translation by C. Gallagher.)

16 Lacan, J., *Le Séminaire, Livre XXII, RSI*, leçon du 21 janvier 1975. (*The Seminar of Jacques Lacan, Book XXII, RSI*, Seminar 4, Tuesday 21 January 1975. Translation by C. Gallagher.)

17 Lacan, J., *Le Séminaire, Livre XXIII, Le sinthome*, p. 94. (*The Sinthome: The Seminar of Jacques Lacan, Book XXIII*. Polity Press, Cambridge, 2018, p. 77. Translation by A.R. Price.)

18 Lacan, J., *Le Séminaire, Livre XXII, RSI*, leçon du 11 février 1975. (*The Seminar of Jacques Lacan Book, XXII, RSI*, Seminar 5, Tuesday 11 February 1975. Translation by C. Gallagher.)

19 Lacan, J., *Le Séminaire, Livre XXII, RSI*, leçon du 8 avril 1975. (*The Seminar of Jacques Lacan Book, XXII, RSI*, Seminar 9. Tuesday 8 April 1975. Translation by C. Gallagher.)
20 Lacan, J., *Le Séminaire, Livre XIII, L'objet de la psychanalyse*, inédit, leçon du 1 juin 1966. (*The Seminar of Jacques Lacan Book XIII, The Object of Psychoanalysis*. Seminar 20. Wednesday 1 June 1966 p. 291. Translation by Cormac Gallagher.)
21 Lacan, J., « Radiophonie », in *Autres écrits*, Paris, le Seuil, 2001, p. 437. (Radiophonie. p. 23. Translation by J.W. Stone.)
22 Lacan, J., *Le Séminaire, Livre XVI, d'Un Autre à l'autre*, p. 281. (*From an Other to the other, The Seminar of Jacques Lacan / Book XVI*, p. 244. Translation by Bruce Fink.)
23 Lacan, J., *Le Séminaire, Livre XVI, d'Un Autre à l'autre*, p. 280 / p. 243 in English translation.
24 Lacan, J., *Le Séminaire, Livre XVI, d'Un Autre à l'autre*, p. 281 / p. 244 in English translation.
25 Lacan, J., « Introduction à l'édition allemande d'un premier volume des *Ecrits* », in *Autres écrits*, p. 557. (*Introduction to a first volume of the* Ecrits (Walter Verlag), published in *Scilicet*, 1975, no. 5, p. 4. Translation by Jack W. Stone.)
26 Lacan, J., « Conférences et entretiens dans des universités nord-américaines », *Scilicet*, no. 6/7, 1975, p. 32. ("Conferences and Conversations at North American Universities.")
27 Lacan, J., *Le Séminaire, Livre XXIV, L'insu que sait de l'une-bévue s'aile à mourre*, leçon du 16 novembre 1976.
28 Lacan, J. Séminaire XXI "Les non-dupes errant", Séance du 9 avril 1974. Inédit. ("Les non-dupes errant", Book XXI, 9 April 1974 Session, p. 189. Translated by C. Gallagher.)
29 Lacan, J., *Le Séminaire, Livre XXIII, Le sinthome*, p. 136. ("Position of the Unconscious", *The Sinthome: The Seminar of Jacques Lacan Book XXIII*. Polity Press, Cambridge, 2018, p. 116. Translation by A.R. Price.)
30 Lacan, J. Séminaire V "Les formations de l'inconscient", Séance du 8 janvier 1958 (The Formations of the Unconscious, Book V, 8th April 1958 Session), pp. 128–140. Translated by C. Gallagher.
31 Lacan, J., *Le Séminaire, Livre XXIII, Le sinthome*, p. 15 / p. 7 in English translation.
32 Lacan, J., *Le Séminaire, Livre XXIII, Le sinthome*, p. 136 / p. 116 in English translation.
33 Lacan, J., *Le Séminaire, Livre XX, Encore*, p. 77. (*The Seminar of Jacques Lacan, Book XX, Encore, 1972–1973*. p. 172. Translation by C. Gallagher.)
34 Lacan, J., *Le Séminaire, Livre XXII, RSI*, leçon du 17 décembre 1974. Author's italics. (*The Seminar of Jacques Lacan Book XXII RSI*, Seminar 2. Tuesday 17 Decembre 1974, p. 46. Translation by C. Gallagher.)

Chapter 6

To Make Use of One's Singularity

"Being heretic in the right way"

Lacan, regarding Joyce, makes use of two combined expressions to report what becomes of the symptom at the end of an analysis, and he introduces the term *sinthome*. That's how, in Joyce's case, he poses that "the nature of the *sinthome* has been recognized, doesn't shrink from using it logically, that is, from using it to the point of reaching the real, at the of which it is sated".[1] Then he also argues that Joyce is "being heretic in the right way".[2] "Using [it] logically" of his symptom, and "being heretic in the right way" are two propositions to be conceived as combined. They are linked to a singular use of the symptom which pushes it to its ultimate consequences, which are that paradoxically the symptom doesn't constitute an impediment for the subject.

The emerging idea is that what is valid for Joyce may be applied to the analytical clinic. It's what we are willing to demonstrate, beginning with the change performed by Lacan who switches it from symptom to *sinthome*. With Freud, we know the substitutive dimension in the symptom, a repression effect. It's the symbolic dimension of symptom as an unconscious formation. After Lacan's reading of it, one brings the real out of the symptom, it's the included dimension of *jouissance*. But what does the real of *sinthome* mean? The real of *sinthome*, with its new reading, it's the reduction of inhibition, of anxiety, and obstacles linked to the symptom. It's not the absence of symptom, but its refinement. It's why in the text "Lituraterre", Lacan makes use of this formulation that he poses as a model for psychoanalysis, when he indicates that Joyce would have gotten nothing more out of a psychoanalysis than what he found by himself: "he would have gained nothing by it, going as he did directly to the best that one can expect of psychoanalysis at its end".[3] Therefore, Lacan doesn't pose what analysis would have done best in this case, it's rather the opposite; he questions how psychoanalysis may learn from the result Joyce obtained without psychoanalysis. Going straight ahead, for Joyce, implies to be unimpeded and to have no obstacle to bypass. This is like "using it logically" of his symptom. Joyce knew where he was heading, there was no hindrance to his writing projects.

DOI: 10.4324/9781003568315-7

He was not incarnating the entangled subject. Therefore, it seems to me that the expression "using it logically" and the expression "being heretic in the right way" are the demonstration of the meaning of the formulation "Father can be bypassed, on the condition that one makes use of it".

Yet, I don't think that Lacan restricts these formulations to psychosis. The term *sinthome*, like that of *substitute*, where the expressions "be bypassed, on the condition that one make use of it", or "being heretic in the right way", are not to be correlated to a clinical structure in particular. That's why one should find out what is meant by, for example "being heretic in the right way" when applied to Joyce. Besides, Lacan said about himself, "But it's a fact that Joyce makes a choice, and in this regard he is, like me, a heretic. One has to choose the path by which to capture the truth".[4]

Let's resume Joyce. There exists a subject's answer which falls under a choice of *jouissance*. Lacan's hint about being heretic indicates it, namely by following the etymology of *heresy*, "choice". Joyce's answer, his choice, is a continuous operation on language [*la langue*]. That's an invention which requires knowledge of how to use it. That's an indication which demonstrates that to bypass the father is something else than to go further than the father. There is a clinical distinction to be made. For Joyce, the efficacy of the invention is due to the fact that he bypassed God and put in his place what was the most suitable to his case. That's what Lacan, about Joyce, describes as being heretic.

So, what would it be to be heretic the right way? Lacan specified it through Joyce's dual choice. First of all, there is the choice to be heretic. In his case, it's a choice of preference as regards a doctrine, that is to say as regards the religious doctrine. The conclusion of *Portrait of the Artist as a Young Man* indicates it. Joyce writes: "I do not want to serve what I no longer believe in. Whether it is called my home, my country, or my church".[5] Therefore here, there is a preference for a renunciation of the religious doctrine. That, is to be heretic. What remains unclear is: what do we mean by "the right way"? That's to identify the nature of one's symptom and make a logical use of it, up to attaining the real. That is Joyce's model. Lacan says it like this: "to take Joyce as a model".[6] That means that he went straight to the real. Therefore, it must be considered that Lacan adds "to make a logical use". Indeed, Joyce never ceased to make a logical use of his symptom. He made the choice to use the *sinthome* to make a logical use of it, and up to the end. Thus, rather than make the choice of religion, he chose to make a name for himself from a literary artwork.

In my opinion, this proposition is on the same line as what Lacan was advancing at that time, when he formulated that "psychoanalysis, when it succeeds, proves that the Name-of-the-Father (*le Nom-du-Père*) can just as well be bypassed [...] on the condition that one make use of it".[7] Therefore, he resumes in 1976 the notion of making use of it, as he made use of it earlier, but differently. Indeed, in 1958 he had already evoked the necessity to make use of the Name-of-the-Father [*le Nom-du-Père*], and here what Lacan is adding is that one may bypass it. What's new in Lacan's proposal is that it focuses on the future of the symptom at the end of an analysis. Therefore, I believe that it's not absurd to argue that this formulation about the symptom applies to the clinic in general.

For both structures of neurosis, hysteria, and obsessional neurosis, it would be to bypass the fantasy linked to the nostalgia of the father, and to cease believing that there is a father who may occupy this place. It would therefore consist of making the choice to cease believing in the One in the Other.

In Freud there exists the idea about the belief of a necessary father, founder of the subject's belief. Therefore "to bypass it", with regard to the father, is not ceasing to believe, but it's to believe the right way. In my opinion, "being heretic the right way" may be defined as the know-how to make use of one's symptom. For instance, some men know how much fuss it may be to believe in *The* woman, nonetheless they can't bypass it. To believe in *The* woman, unfolds in several ways. There are some men for whom it is enough that someone be among the female gender, to make them believe her. Only one woman is enough, and so when she says something, one believes her, since it's her who says it. To be more specific, clinically, it occurs with men in analysis through the complaint: "It's as if I was listening my wife's voice." Therefore, that is precisely the dimension of believing her, it's almost picking out a woman's words as being an injunction. And so, for a man it may take the form of a quasi-hallucinatory superego, that he put outside himself. To move from believing in *The* woman to a know-how with a woman, has to be correlated with being heretic the right way. What do we mean by a know-how with a woman? It's at least to introduce a distance with her "spoken words" [*ses dits*], and to take them as being the speaking truth.

On the female side, it's not about believing in the man, it's to bypass the belief in the "Man". When Lacan writes the "Man" with a capital M, it's to display the hysterical position which consists of believing that "at least one" has got to exist. Lacan makes a pun with man and at-least-one, and write it like this in French: "*l'Homoinzin*". That would be *l'au-moins-un* [at-least-one] who escapes castration. However, it's certain that in the course of an analysis, the belief in the existence of this *"au-moins-un"* [at-least-one] drops. This is what at the same time is having the effect of being able to switch to the relation with a man. Capital M doesn't exist, but men exist. Therefore, in a way, analysis facilitates the conditions of encounter. But I think that for a woman, this is not the proper formulation for "being heretic the right way", but instead it is to cease believing in *The* woman. One could say it is the same for a man: in both cases, it is imperative to cease believing in *The* woman. That's a fact. However, for a woman, the other woman doesn't possess a voice which would be of the order of an injunction. But there is a belief that the woman is the Other. One finds the idea that in this case there is the One in the Other.

The subject, after the analysis, knows how to make use of this belief. Why don't we eventually say that it's reciprocal and, as for the man, the issue would be to bypass the belief in *The* woman, and for a woman it would be to bypass the belief in *The* man? For a fundamental reason – it's a clinical fact which responds to the oedipal asymmetry – a woman sets her mother in a position to be an Other who occupies a place which is always the Other's place. For a woman, it's complicated to become heretic of one's own mother, therefore it's difficult to bypass her. A woman may make use of it and cope with the mother, but she never fully parts with her.

To return to Joyce, one may argue that he bypasses the hypothesis of God. In that sense, one may also argue that there is an analytical effect which could be called the analytical heresy, which consists of bypassing the hypothesis of God in favor of the hypothesis of the unconscious. It's an ethical choice for the subjects who have completed their analysis. One doesn't bypass the unconscious, one draws consequences of its effect, of one's relationship with one's unconscious. That is precisely – in my opinion – at the end of an analysis, when one may qualify as being heretic the right way.

We may, with Joyce, ask ourselves the question of the woman's place. According to the biographers' statements, Nora has been the unique woman in his life. That's true too, that some people talk about a few liaisons he would have had. However, in all his life the relation that mattered was Nora's. Therefore, which status may we give to Nora? Lacan says: "she fits him as a glove".[8] One realizes that it's not in the same vein as knowing how to make use of the symptom with the woman. To fit him as a glove means that she perfectly adapted to him, that she knew how to manage exactly what was suiting him. Therefore, it would be a woman who would incarnate the acme of what would be an accommodating woman. Let's notice that Lacan formulated, as follows the bond a woman could have to the man, by being accommodating:

> Hence the universal of what women desire is sheer madness: all women are mad, they say. That's precisely why they are not-all, that is to say not-at-all-mad-about-the-whole; accommodating rather: to the point where there is no limit to the concessions made by any woman for *a* man: of her body, her soul, her possessions.[9]

Nora incarnates, according to what we may deduce from her biography and Joyce's one, the absence of limits as to concessions. We can make the hypothesis that she had been pushed from a position of being "rather accommodating" to that of becoming the pure accommodating. Therefore, it was not Joyce who put Nora in the position to be his symptom, it was rather the opposite. It's Nora who understood what was necessary to Joyce and made the best of it. Therefore, she certainly had a function of the necessary support he needed. Thus, she participated in the substitute he invented to compensate the paternal deficiency. Surely, Lacan demonstrates the necessary function of writing, but we may hypothesize that writing alone would not have been enough. What must also be considered is what has been the function of publication, then the place of his wife. Therefore, it's certain that Nora participated in Joyce's subjective stability.

The choice of the symptom

In order to carry on discussing what constitutes the essence of the analytical clinic, it seems necessary to return to the analytical symptom. Lacan's thesis about the symptom is consistent with Freud's development, to the extent that Lacan puts forward a structural deficit regarding the possibility *de jouir* [to rejoice]. There is a global lack regarding the *jouissance*. If all the subjects are concerned, it's because of the subtraction of *jouissance* carried out by the language. This lack needs to be compensated. It's where arises the function of the symptom for everyone.

To this fact is joining another one. All of these clinical structures have this in common, that this lack-of-*jouissance* [*manque-à-jouir*] is attributed to the Other. At the start, as early as the subject's first childhood experiences of satisfaction, there is the assumption of something wrong. It's consistent with Freud's proposition, which sustains the notion of a never-disappearing culpability. It was a way to sustain a widespread lack-of-*jouissance* [*manque-à-jouir*]. Besides, with the myth in *Totem and Taboo*, Freud poses for every subject the existence of an all-mighty-father. It would be the man with an absolute power, limitless in his relation to the *jouissance*, and thus able to possess all women. An exceptional man. This is formulated as being a non-impeded [*non-barrée*] *jouissance*. Of course, it doesn't exist, but the subject makes it alive via his fantasy. In a way, for Lacan it means resuming the Freudian thesis, namely that religion is an extension of the father. And religion grabs the notion of culpability, via another angle, with the idea of original sin. Thus, religion captures a structural fact. The subject takes over, through the idea of guilt, the lack-of-*jouissance* [*le manque-à-jouir*]. Therefore, there are two inseparable dimensions: the existence of guilt and the attribution of the lack-of-*jouissance* [*le manque-à-jo*uir], that the subject attributes to the Other.

It's appropriate to realize that on this point Lacan breaks away from Freud, denouncing what he calls "crucial problems for psychoanalysis", the original sin of psychoanalysis. He defines it as being Freud's desire to reintroduce God. Why reintroduce God? It's because, one could think that God got out of the structure and that it was Freud who had reintroduced Him. It's where the formulation "being heretic the right way" was taking even more value. It's a way to cease attributing the *jouissance* to God. To cease attributing to God the creation of the world, and do as Joyce did: he attributed the creation to himself. It's where it means "make use of it" about the symptom. This is like making use of the *jouissance* of one's symptom. In this sense, it can be generalized, it takes over the *jouissance* which locates itself in the true hole, the hole of the subject's structure. Therefore, the Joycean heresy does without the hypothesis of God.

The analytical heresy is to bypass the hypothesis of God, by supporting the hypothesis of the unconscious. Therefore here, there's an ethical choice. It's a fact that there exists a failure inside the structure. That's a failure which is confirmed for all of us. This failure, Lacan called a "slip of the knot". He formalized it with knots he called Borromean, and posed the idea of the existence of a slip at the level of a knot, which must be repaired. Therefore, it's precisely where religion is standing. Religion, thank God, repairs the knot at the level of a slip. It's precisely where the analytical promise occurs and what I evoked as being the possibility to produce a viable atheist.

That's a way to cease attributing to God the *jouissance* which doesn't exist. It's ceasing to localize it at the level of God. As Lacan formulates it in *Encore*, God and *The* woman come at the same place. It's precisely where one must revert to the formulation "to bypass The-Name-of-the-Father on the condition that one make use of it". Lacan introduces this formulation via the already evoked sentence: "Psychoanalysis, when it succeeds, proves that the Name-of-the-Father can just as well be bypassed [...] on the condition that one make use of it".[10] When he says "psychoanalysis [...] proves", I'm inclined to sustain that it only takes one successful case to allow oneself to say that psychoanalysis is successful. Therefore, one doesn't need a whole series of statistical cases to prove psychoanalysis' success. Therefore, one assumes that analysis can succeed only out of one successful case.

Therefore, analysand and analyst make the assumption of success, and precisely there, the analyst has his share of responsibility. From the outset the question is, does he or does he not involve someone in an analysis? However, the supposition of success is one thing, the result is quite another. Supposition concerns the entry in analysis. The conclusion of the supposition, which as well is just the analysis result, is to cease believing, to cease the supposition. Nevertheless, by the end the conclusion of the supposition does not end with transference via negative transference. Negative transference is a way to maintain God. It's about aiming to reach the real of the symptom, its irreducibility, what indicates that at the end – no more than at the outset – one is not free, since one is determined by one's symptom. To switch from belief in the Other to belief in one's symptom, falls under an ethical choice. It's switching the One into the Other, to believe in the One per se. Let's set apart belief in the symptom at the outset of the analysis, to what becomes of that belief at the end of the cure. At the outset, to believe in the analytical symptom means to believe that it's meaningful, that it includes a message to decipher. At the end, once the rounds of its meaning have been made, remains a belief that the symptom reduced to its nucleus of real is what makes someone's case, unlike the others. It's the belief in singularity.

One can't raise these questions without referring to wandering. Lacan in *Anxiety* makes some remarks where he indicates phenomena which are a clue to wandering. That's the case of the runaway, figured out as a passage to the act. These are quests to find a way outside the symbolic. Therefore, it's important to know to what extent an exit out of the symbolic is or is not reversable. A reversable exit of the symbolic, it's an *acting out* (emphasis in original), an irreversible exit, a non-return one, is this wandering in the real, what one identifies as a passage to the act. Here, it's necessary to make a distinction between wandering and exile. Lacan gives a definition of exile when he evokes "our *jouissance* going off the track".[11] Going off the track is to pass by the *jouissance* that one hopes for, and remain disappointed. Disappointment about the *jouissance* is a sign of the belief to be able to reach the *jouissance*, whereas there is no other possibility than to encounter the limits. The subject experiences that he passed by, he remains excluded, he is exiled. It can be declined in different ways which are other ways of saying that the subject is undocked from the *jouissance*. That's what very early on Lacan puts forward, as a hole in the structure, a traumatic hole because of language, which leaves the subject in a definitive exclusion. It's what is meant by the *troumatisme* [a pun built on: *trou* = hole + *traumatisme* = traumatism]. Therefrom, the necessity for subjects to fill this hole. They fill it by producing some romances, they redraft afterwards. It's what Freud evoked as "the neurotic's family romance"; which doesn't exclude psychosis, since it refers to the psychotic subject's delusional romance. Therefore, by its very nature, the subject participates with a dimension in relation to the *jouissance*, from which he is excluded because of the signifier, which introduces a disjunction between want and satisfaction. When one speaks about satisfaction of the want, one is in a direct link. It's exclusively possible for animals. For the speaking being, from the time that language seeps through, the exclusion of *jouissance* is programmed. Therefore, there exists an initial form of exclusion, it's the exclusion of nature due to language, and therefore the birth of the drive. Another form of exclusion, also linked to the input of language into the body, is the *jouissance*.

Then what are the modalities of doing with regard to the exclusion? When Lacan proposes the Name-of-the-Father [*le Nom-du-Père*], with this signifier he introduces a know-how facing the Other's *jouissance*. Psychotic wandering is something else, it's the wandering of a free man that nothing can settle. There is no localization of *jouissance*; it lacks the possibility to name the other's *jouissance*. The subject is compelled to bring back all his interpretations to a unique interpretation: "The Other wants *jouir* [to rejoice] of me".

To make oneself a good dupe

Besides, it's appropriate to clinically differentiate psychotic wandering from hysteric wandering. Lacan evokes in *The Formations of the Unconscious* that a true femininity has also, a little, a dimension of alibi. "Real women always have something a little bit astray about them".[12] That a true woman possesses something a little bit astray, is a way to formulate that she is not completely caught up in the phallic function. There is a wandering inherent to being-a-woman and her position not-all-of-it in her relation to the phallus. But more broadly, it's appropriate to notice that there is a structural flaw concerning the subject's structuring. It is related to the lack of a signifier in the Other which leads to what Lacan designated as the "slip of the knot", indicating the error in the structure. What becomes essential is each one's compass to find a way regarding this error. Lacan occasionally evokes the psychoanalyst's wandering. That would be that of not finding his way with his act. Lacan might have spoken of Freud's wandering. In *RSI*, he evoked Freud's attempt to make the analytic discourse completely adequate to the scientific discourse. Lacan had, very early on, concluded that psychoanalysis was not a science. Therefrom, the notion of wandering about Freud: "that is his erring". Freud's erring is to overlook that there is a dimension which creates the real of the analytical experience. To believe in the scientific discourse, is to believe exclusively in the facts. That's why Lacan in "Les non-dupes errent" [the non-dupes who err], evokes "the good dupe" [*la bonne dupe*]. "The good dupe" is ultimately a way to resume "to believe or not", and at the end of an analysis to know what you believe in. Lacan gives this definition: "the good dupe, the one who does not err, must have somewhere a Real of which she is the dupe".[13] In other words, one may say that the end of an analysis means believing in the real in the subject. It's appropriate to differentiate a real with direction and a real without. The wandering example gives the idea of a real being adrift.

There is a real of orientation, "The good dupe", the good belief at the end of an analysis, which is the opposite of wandering, it is to access the compass which avoids erring. Therefore, there is a belief which ends after the end of an analysis and then there is an effect of "being dupe" of a real. Which real? Each one's real, not a real external to the subject. But to achieve it, the subject's link to his love for his unconscious must be considered. As Lacan says it: "who is not in love with his unconscious errs".[14] Therefore, Lacan reiterates Freud's proposition about love and the change one may expect out of a completed analysis.

One can also find that in this interesting formulation when Lacan says: "Love is nothing more than a saying, *qua* happening. A happening without any burrs".[15] A saying is what exists with regard to the "spoken word" [*le dit*]. You have to refer to the "spoken word" [*le dit*] and to the saying [*le dire*] as a couple.[16] In analysis, there is the set of things formulated by the analysand, and also what he does not say, but which is commanding his sayings [*dires*]. Therefore, a saying exists. It ex-ists [*il existe*], as Lacan writes it; it means that it exists outside, one cannot grasp it, one cannot grab it; one may potentially interpret it. You have got to have an interpretation of the Other to say: "that, it is the saying (*le dire*)." That's why Lacan condenses the whole of Freud's "spoken words" [*des dits*] about sexuality within a formulation which demonstrates the whole of his "spoken words" [*ses dits*]. Therefore, "there is no such thing as a sexual relationship", that is Freud's saying [*dire*] about sexuality. The saying [*le dire*] in analysis, it is a real resource for the "spoken word" [*le dit*], but unutterable. The "spoken words" [*les dits*], therefore the whole of a subject's statements, are about the subject's relationship to the truth, even if somethings escape it. That is the *mi-dit* [half-spoken] truth. Lacan formulates it otherwise when he poses that truth is "sister of [...] enjoyment".[17] One grasps a part of truth, the other, one does not capture it since it is of the order of the *jouissance*. Let's get back to the question of "Love [...] A happening without any burrs". First of all, to pose love in terms of saying [*dire*], puts love into another dimension than those of the "spoken words about love" [*les dits de l'amour*]. Let's take the most frequent "spoken words" [*les dits*]: "I love you, you love me", etc. obviously they fall under the most common type of language, but do they indicate any affect which would be a real? Likewise, the love of truth. If one connects this love with the fact that truth is lying, as Lacan formulated it, one notices the need to differentiate fictitious love from true love. Therefrom, the question is about a love which would not be a semblance, and which would not be only a passion for truth.

What is meant by that term of burr [*bavure*]? On Wiktionary, one may find the following definition: "A small piece of material left on an edge after a cutting operation".[18] How not to see that love without burrs is as a love uncontaminated by smudges or stains. It would be what's left of love once the stains of the imaginary had been removed. It would be a love as close as possible to the real.

Thus, a love being as an affect of the real would be something else than an affect submitted to contradiction. Love-contradiction is the one that one observes when one believes in true love, and after a while, sometimes without any real reason, one is immersed in a feeling of disillusionment. How could love be different as being "a saying [*dire*] without any burrs"? In my opinion, burrs have something to do with chatter [*bavardage*]. Thus, it gets back to Lacan's formulation: "love more worthy than the proliferation of chatter".[19] It is rising love to a dignity other than that of a speech about love, which as such is not binding.

Therefore, love without burr is love without chatter. Thus, we are on the side of what would be a true love, that is to say a love which would not go through the "spoken word" [*le dit*], and which would be about experience, which is transmitted, which is recognized through the other's unconscious. A love which resonates within the other without any necessity to formulate a request for love.

Besides, it is funny the way Lacan refers to an irresistible formulation able to arouse love out of the other, and he says that it may be non-articulatable, even if it is articulated, namely: "I desire you, even if I do not know it".[20] One realizes that if there is a chance to arouse love, it is not through a request. To request love never brought forth love.

It is why, when Lacan evokes a love encounter, he puts forward the following formulation: "The encounter, it must indeed be said, of symptoms, of affects, of that which in each individual marks the trace of his exile, not as a subject, but as speaking, of his exile from this relationship".[21] In other words, all of us are exiled from non-existent sexual relationships, for lack of writing in the unconscious. What remains is the possibility of an encounter, and it is why Lacan evoking love as "a *dire* without any burrs" evokes the event. It is the encounter of symptoms, affects, of what in everyone marks the trace of one's exile. In another words, love-encounter is an encounter between two exiles who make resonate their symptoms. Lacan does not speak about the encounter in the love partner; he refers to the encounter of symptoms and affects. Naturally, the affect includes the dimension of love, but there must be something which is of the order of an encounter between two symptoms, and when one evokes two symptoms, one is evoking two modalities of *jouissance* which encounter via what resonates out of their unconscious. That is to say, that the first one's unconscious resonates with the other's, via a symptomatic resonance. It is what produces the event of love when it does not limit itself to its imaginary mirage.

Psychoanalysis does not promise love-encounter at the end of the analysis; there are subjects who end the analysis and have not encountered their partner in symptom. There are subjects who sometimes encounter theirs a long time after the end of the analysis, and there are subjects who modify their relationship to their partner, in order to organize differently the symptoms between the subject and his partner. Therefore, the end of analysis does not necessarily involve a change of partner, but still what is required from the subject, is at least in his relationship to be obsessed with a belief in love. What can be deduced from Lacan's proposition is that love at the end of an analysis does not sustain itself with a belief, nor a delusion, but with the other's symptom encounter, which requires courage. Therefore, it requires courage, not only with regard to one's own symptom, but also towards the other's symptom.

The *dire* of a case

What makes the case in analysis, is not the whole of a subject's "spoken words" [*les dits*], but his saying [*dire*]. The analyst may have an idea about a subject's saying [*dire*], but what is really attesting of a saying [*dire*] is what remains of the analysis when it has been brought to an end. Thus, one cannot assert the saying [*dire*] of the case without the analyst's saying [*dire*]. When one says "a saying" [*un dire*], one is in the dimension of an event, something which happens, which is not temporary, rather something writing itself for the subject. It is in this sense that one can say that the saying [*dire*] is what ex-sists [*ex-siste*] for the *dits* [spoken words]. The saying [*dire*] participates in a real. For example, there is no saying [*dire*] for an autist. For him, within his statements, it is only an arrangement of words. They may possess a meaning, even a sense, but without coupling to a saying [*dire*]. It is also the case with the schizophrenic. On the other hand, when one is in the "spoken words" [*les dits*], one is in the dimension of truth, namely that, with the "spoken words" [*les dits*], one tries to grab what could be the truth, but truth does not catch the saying [*dire*]. It stays short of it.

There is no doubt that when one analyzes, one begins with a subject's "spoken words" [*les dits*] with the aim of deciphering the unconscious, and the meaning of the analyst's interpretation is the quest of truth. It happens at the subject's level. What must be noticed, is that Lacan did not stop there. If he introduces the *parlêtre* [speaking-being] notion, it is because he moved beyond the question of the subject. The *parlêtre* [speaking-being] is the speaking body. When one analyzes in the light of the *parlêtre* [speaking-being], the interpretation does not aim at the truth, but at the *jouissance*. In this sense, I believe that Lacan, once he introduces the *parlêtre* [speaking-being], draws consequences for his conception of the subject. A conception of analysis which considers the subject with regard to the body's *jouissance*, involves necessarily an update of the practice of interpretation. With the term of *parlêtre* [speaking-being], one is not in a theoretical sophistication. The practice of interpretation is not the same if one considers the subject as traversed by signifiers and considers the speaking body. Therefore, for Lacan there is a shift in the orientation of an analysis, from truth to *jouissance*. *Jouissance* does not exclude the search for truth, as long as one is informed that one does not grasp the ultimate truth. Therefore, from the introduction of the term *parlêtre* [speaking-being], the analytical practice becomes a practice aiming at the subject's *jouissance*.

What is becomes of the symptom at the end of analysis? The symptom becomes the sense of the real. One often opposes sense and real. That is simply due to the fact that Lacan formulates the real as a *a-version* [in two words: meaning aversion in English], with regard to the sense. It poses that one catches the real once the sense is being cleared out. Sense and real are therefore in opposition. To give sense to the symptom does not mean considering the real. It gives an idea of an analytical practice focused onto the sense. However, the question is to know if a practice which takes the real into consideration means that it does not bother with the sense. It seems to me that it's worth questioning the notion of the real sense of the symptom.

There is a real of symptom, it is the undecipherable mark; what remains of the symptom after an effort of elucidation in analysis. This real is called the fool's sense [*le sens de l'insensé*]. It is not a sense which can be shared. This is not a common sense. The sense of symptom is given by this real and by the absence of sexual relationship. It is precisely there, at that spot of absence, that the symptom locates itself as being what has been written in lieu of a hole. For a subject, the symptom is always a substitute for the inexistence of sexual relationship, or "lack-of-meaning" [*l'ab-sence*]. "The lack-of-sex-meaning" [*l'absexe*], as Lacan says, referring to Freud: "Freud puts us on the track of the fact that lack-of-meaning *(ab-sens)* designates sex: it is by the inflation of this lack-of-sex-meaning *(sens-absexe)* that a topology is unfolded where it is the word that decides".[22] If Freud helps us in that regard, it is because he indicated that at the level of the unconscious is missing the inscription of the gender difference.

The analysand's saying [*dire*] lies behind the whole of its demands. There is a real sense to this demand. Where does it come from? There is a real sense of the saying [*le dire*] of the analysis demand. You think you'll be able to grab it by the exhaustion of the object's metonymy. The demand would manifest itself through the quest of an object of satisfaction and it is precisely there that occurs the metonymy. The demand would be to obtain the object of dreams, but the experience confronts the subject with a "it's not that". One does not grab the real via metonymy, but because of the analytical interpretation aiming the subject's One, the One being each one's proper real. In "L'étourdit", Lacan evokes the fact that "the dialogue between one sex and the other being forbidden [...] there results some difficulty in dialogue within each sex".[23] For the analytical clinic, it resumes the idea of not trying to understand. Each one, when one tries to make use of signifiers, does it with regards to one's own experience and this invalidates the whole idea of trying to put oneself in somebody else's place.

It conveys fundamental consequences for the analytical practice. No dialogue: not only between genders and within the same gender, but also in Lacan, between analysand and analyst. No dialogue as a real for the speaking one. It indicates the place of the limit in the interpretation. As long as one believes in dialogue, there is a real which escapes. One grabs the real via interpretation. It is the analytical interpretation which makes sure to put a limit to this no-dialogue, in other words to put precisely at this place what analysand and analyst encounter as a real. "This no-dialogue has its limit within interpretation, through which is ascertained the [...] real."[24]

The analytical interpretation not only conditions the subject's associations, but also the encounter with the real. Interpretation therefore aims the real and involves necessarily a statement which has to be sustained by a saying [*un dire*]. It is precisely what the analyst does not say but which orders the "spoken word" [*le dit*], as it is the case to say everything. The analyst's saying [*dire*] is a silent one. What is the silent saying's [*le dire*] purpose, not to be confused with a silent analyst?

A first finality is to show that there is something beyond the passion for truth. There are several relations to the truth. There are those who more or less looks for it, those who reject it, but there is a clinical structure which is marked by the passion for truth: it is hysteria. It is why sometimes analyses linger and do not come to their end. There is always a remnant of this passion for truth which revives the free association. Therefore, the analyst's silent saying [*dire*] opens up to something beyond this passion for truth, since this acting saying [*dire*] makes the analysand feel that this passion, like all passion, includes a painful dimension. Necessarily, to go beyond truth does not happen without some loss. An analysis includes the programmed encounter with disappointment. It is subjective and linked to some expectations. It is also linked to transference and downfall of the ideal. Then, there is also for trainee analysts the encounter with the limits of psychoanalysis practice. One may see it in some controls where the analyst tends to put himself in the analysand's shoes and asks the question "what can I do for you?"

I evoked the transference disappointment. The programmed disappointment of the non-supposition of knowledge regarding the analyst, is a downfall of transference. There is a dimension which changes towards the analyst and it is the transformation of the love of transference. Freud evokes it in his conclusive text "Analysis Terminable and Interminable". He does not say "or", but "and". It is to say that there is something which terminates itself and something which does not. That goes for transference. The rest of Freud's text makes possible, for a number of cases, and from his experience, that the analysis ends by a kind of friendship between the analysand and the analyst. Friendship is a kind of love. There is a transformation of the love of transference. That is not all-or-nothing. That is also the reason why, about transference, the term of *liquidation* is inappropriate. One ends one's analysis and one is related to a few others. One keeps on reading, working with others with whom one is in transference. According to Freud, there is a link which goes on differently.

Clinic of the *jouissance*

In "The Direction of the Treatment and the Principles of its Power", to evoke the psychoanalysis policy, Lacan states "the lack-of-being policy". It has to be distinguished from the subject's lack-of-being at the beginning of an analysis. Indeed, so that there is a beginning in analysis, the subject has to confront a lack at the level of his being. The paradox is that one demands a complement of being to someone whose policy is to establish a practice based upon the lack-of-being. The analysand's lack-of-being however is not the same as the analyst's policy. This lack-of-being is possible if, besides, the analyst has been able to access a subject possessing a surplus of being, acquired in his own experience as an analysand. The lack-of-being policy is a draft to what afterwards Lacan calls "the analyst's desire". The lack-of-being, which is for the subject a negative feeling, nonetheless is a condition of desire. It is only from a lack that one desires. Therefore, the lack-of-being policy implies that analysis practice aims to look out for the lack as a condition for producing a desire. On the other hand, if Lacan speaks about a lack-of-being policy, it is to radically erase the notion of counter-transference. Lack-of-being policy highlights the fact that the analyst is not a subject by the time he operates as analyst. Rather what is required from the one who holds this place is to have cleared one's mind of prejudices regarding a subject's choices for his existence.

That is what afterwards Lacan formulates in terms of "object *a* semblance". There is a logic coherence. "Object *a* semblance" indicates the existence of an object, precisely where the analyst cannot take a stand as a subject. If he positions himself as a subject, he promotes the identification. The only weapon, to avoid identification, and which does not intervene at the end, is the analyst as an "object *a* semblance". That is precisely where the case-based clinic reveals itself. The analyst as an "object *a* semblance" promotes a policy of singularity.

Lack-of-being policy is, as it is in "The Direction of the Treatment and the Principles of its Power", an answer to Ferenczy who addresses the issue as "how to act with one's being", in reference to the analyst's being in the treatment.[25] Lacan's objection to this position is in the lack-of-being as the analyst's policy. The analyst's being has no place in the treatment, and manifestations of the analyst's being should not interfere with it. Here, it is interesting, to resume Lacan's terms when he answers to Sacha Nacht in his "Preface to the English-Language edition of *Seminar XI*". Lacan denounces Nacht's statements which support the doctrine of an innate psychoanalyst's being. Lacan objects: one is not an inborn psychoanalyst, "a certificate tells me that I was born. I repudiate this certificate".[26] The analyst's desire, answers Lacan, is a production. For someone who goes through the analysis experience, the analyst is an effect. Indeed, in an analyst's production, there is an effect which is equivalent to what Lacan evoked about Joyce in terms of "a cancelled subscription to the unconscious".[27] The analyst, when he operates, is "a cancelled subscription to the unconscious". It is coherent with the lack-of-being.

Sometimes during a control, analysts while speaking about a case, formulate: "it touched me". When one is touched, one is not "a cancelled subscription to the unconscious", one is in connection with one's own unconscious, and what one is saying the subject may resonate with one's own unconscious. The analyst when he operates has dismissed his unconscious. It is central to evoke what one may expect from an analysis.

There is what each subject expects as soon as he addresses his first demands to the analyst. There is also what a subject may expect as he proceeds through the treatment. Often, there are new expectations. They are linked to analysis discoveries which bring out unexpected desires. Then, there is what the analyst may expect out of an analysis. That is where precisely the case-based clinic becomes crucial. For, it is not the same, what one may expect out of a case-based clinic, and what one may expect out of a clinic of the *jouissance*.

The clinic of subject is a clinic of desire; it aims at its elucidation. The case-based clinic supposes the clinic of a particular modality aiming to do with the *jouissance*. Let's take the case of hysteria. In the clinic of subject, one elucidates the paradoxes of desire via disidentification, which enable to give free rein to the man [*lâcher la pente à faire l'homme*] or to bring into ex-istence [*faire ex-ister*], the at-least-one-of-exception, that is to say that someone embodies the exception, the One of exception who is not castrated. That is the structural way to become the add-in which is missing to the father. It is structural since one finds it in all cases of hysteria.

But the case-based clinic supposes the clinic of a particular modality to cope with symptom. Thus, the case-based clinic aims to modify the subject's relationship to the *jouissance*. It is precisely there that it is important to return to the definition of the symptom as a body event. The body event is precisely what makes symptom in the subject's structure. Then, there is an analytical body event. It is from his analysis what makes a mark for a hysteric subject. There is therefore, what makes an event for a hysteric subject, his symptom. And there is what Lacan designates as "the frame", that is to say the specificity, the trait which brings the mark to the structure. It is the love of the father. Each time someone refers to a hysteric subject, one could highlight the love of the father. This love of the father constitutes the source of the love for the dead father or the castrated lover. There is a common point to both of them. The subject has to occupy the place of the other's missing object. It's a way of saying that the condition for the hysteric's desire is to be the other's unique object of desire. That is the meaning of the dead father. It is a father who turns a blind eye to the desire. When one takes this conception and its clinical effects, one highlights the relationship to the castration, and its avoidance. The hysteric singularizes castration on the man's side. She is more at ease to make it so that the imaginary castration be on the other's side than on her side. Thus, the unsatisfaction complaint about castration, the hysteric put it on the other's side. If the hysteric is unsatisfied, it is because the other does not know how to satisfy her. It does not constitute a paradox with regard to the fact that often the hysteric appears as missing. It's one thing to show the imaginary castration, that is the display up to the exhibition of the lack, and another thing to assume the symbolic castration, the one relative to which the hysteric is not truly concerned.

You can see the difference in the hysteric's lack-of-being and the analyst's lack-of-being policy. To the analyst, this policy acting as a compass for analysis is what enables that "object *a*" the other desires, to find a place there. The hysteric's lack-of-being is unique in that she would like to make her lack-of-being be a cause of the other's desire. It is in the service of this policy that is working the strategy of the hysteric's unsatisfaction. She does not look for the object of satisfaction, but rather makes herself the cause of the other's desire, in other words, makes it so that her lack-of-being is worth the truth of desire. Thus, on her side she attempts to incarnate the *agalma*. The analyst also positions on his side the "object *a*", but to cause the analysand's desire. A desire which carries the subject elsewhere. Thus, the hysteric is marked by the love of truth. The question is: what is the turning point in the analytical clinic? One may conceive it like this: the more she gives way to the love of the One [*l'amour de l'Un*], the more she makes herself eager. And the more she makes herself eager, the less her desire is for the love for the other's cause.

One could say that she goes from desiring to be desired, to desiring without any scheme. Obviously, occasionally it could also be desiring to be a man's object of desire. In the meantime, what is changing is that the desire is no longer conditioned by a man's love. For to desire, being loved is not required.

Let's return to the analysis policy. It is interesting to follow the change Lacan is operating in his conception of interpretation. For a while, his idea is that interpretation aims to reveal, to unveil, to welcome something new. But there is a turning point. It begins to change when Lacan formulates that interpretation aims at the cause of desire. One deduces from the extent of this modality of interpretation that what matters is the analysand's relationship to the cause of his desire. The real turning point is to go through castration or not. If Lacan evokes a possible path, it is because it is possible to take a stand as a subject, beyond castration. That is precisely where a chance exists for the hysteric subject, when it is a woman, to obtain as a woman a bit more of substance, whereas for a very long time she was believing that it was another woman who embodied this bit more of substance.

I evoked the fact of giving up the quest of love. It is a beneficial effect of castration, for as a result it has the production of an impossible. To consent to the impossible is what enables one to make an end to the quest of the absolute which is always a cause of helplessness. That enables one to say that the analysis solution is not a phallic solution. It is rather to consent to what does not exist. It enables one to measure the gap with the hysteric's position. The hysteric establishes herself as a woman in the other's time. That is precisely what makes her occupy the place of object in the other's fantasy. To cease to be in the other's time, to be in one's own time, is to make the choice to look after the object which is the cause of one's desire. Lacan says it differently in "time to conclude", which enables one to deduce that the end of the analysis has strictly nothing to do with any particular norm; one does not promise any encounter with a partner, nor any solution according to social norm, but by his terms "to know how to handle sexuality". In this proposition there is no requirement, no mention of a partner, no comment about homosexuality, or family, and of course either about transsexuality. It gives us the idea that in the Lacanian analysis there is an analysis with an end: "to know how to handle sexuality". It is what is invented for each subject as an answer in analysis. That is an answer which is not standardized.

And it enables one to attest to what an analysis has produced as *a-norm*. I think that to know how to handle sexuality constitutes the extension to Lacan's question being formulated out of Joyce: "How can an art target in an expressly divinatory way the substantialization of the sinthome in its consistence, but also in its ex-istence and in its hole?"[28] This question has to be considered from Freud's proposition resumed by Lacan, according to which the artist precedes the psychoanalyst. Indeed, Joyce attests to what is meant by a singularity led so far as to incarnate the solution to the hole in the structure.

For psychoanalysis, it would be what constitutes a case, namely, how via the *sinthome*, the subject succeeded to find the substance enabling the knotting of the structure the Borromean way. It is why at the start of an analysis, one cannot promise anything, for one does not know if the subject will know how to handle sexuality. That is undecidable. It is only by the end of an analysis that it may emerge, and it is precisely there that it is decisive to recognize what has been a clinic oriented by the case. To know how to handle one's sexuality, is something else than the link with the sexual partner. This know-how to handle supposes in an analysis, to have taken into consideration the symptom exception which is always sexual.

But to take it into consideration, on the analyst's side, is not merely to draw up a report. It is to take note of the result of an operation of intrusion into the subject's real. One could conclude as follows: the clinic of subject does without the analyst as subject, provided that the analyst's desire be in the right place.

The case-based clinic, as a clinic of the real is a clinic *à deux*. Not two subjects, but two partners of *jouissance*. Nonetheless, with a fundamental difference between them. The analysand is in the *jouissance* of the speech, throughout the analysis. The analyst makes himself the partner of the *jouissance* but with the difference that his speech is emptied of *jouissance*. That is what can be hoped for and therefore required from an analyst.

Notes

1 Lacan, J., *Le Séminaire, Livre XXIII, Le sinthome* p. 15. ("Position of the Unconscious", *The Sinthome The Seminar of Jacques Lacan Book XXIII*. Polity Press, Cambridge, 2018, p. 7. Translation by A.R. Price.)
2 Lacan, J., *Le Séminaire, Livre XXIII, Le sinthome* p. 15 / p. 7 in the English translation.
3 Lacan, J., « Litturaterre », in *Autres écrits*, p. 11. ("Litturaterre", Seminar XVIII p. 4. Translation by J. Stone.)
4 Lacan, J., « Litturaterre », in *Autres écrits,* p. 15 / p. 7 in the English translation.
5 I have translated this from the French edition of the novel. The similar, original sentence can be found in: Joyce, J. *A Portrait of the Artist as a Young Man*, New York, B.W Huebsch, 1916, p. 291.

6 Lacan, J., *Le Séminaire, Livre XXIII, Le sinthome*, p. 164. ("Joyce the Symptom", *The Sinthome: The Seminar of Jacques Lacan Book XXIII*. Polity Press, Cambridge, 2018, p. 144. Translation by A.R. Price.)

7 Lacan, J., *Le Séminaire, Livre XXIII, Le sinthome* p. 136. ("Position of the Unconscious", *The Sinthome: The Seminar of Jacques Lacan Book XXIII*. Polity Press, Cambridge, 2018, p. 116. Translation by A.R. Price.)

8 Lacan, J., *Le Séminaire, Livre XXIII, Le sinthome*, p. 164. ("Joyce the Symptom", *The Sinthome: The Seminar of Jacques Lacan Book XXIII*. Polity Press, Cambridge, 2018, p. 144. Translation by A.R. Price.)

9 Lacan, J., « Télévision », in *Autres écrits*, p. 540. (Television, A Challenge to the Psychoanalytic Establishment", p. 40. W.W. Norton & Company, New York and London. Translation by D. Hollier, R. Krauss, and A. Michelson.)

10 Lacan, J., *Le Séminaire, Livre XXIII, Le sinthome* p. 136. ("Position of the Unconscious", *The Sinthome: The Seminar of Jacques Lacan Book XXIII*. Polity Press, Cambridge, 2018, p. 116. Translation by A.R. Price.)

11 Lacan, J., « Télévision », in *Autres écrits*, p. 534. ("Television, A Challenge to the Psychoanalytic Establishment", p. 32. W.W. Norton & Company. New York and London. Translation by D. Hollier, R. Krauss, and A. Michelson.)

12 Lacan, J., *Le Séminaire, Livre V. Les formations de l'inconscient*, p. 195. (*The Seminar Book V: The Formations of the Unconscious*, p. 173. Translation by Cormac Gallagher.)

13 Lacan, J., *Le Séminaire, Livre XXI. Les non-dupes errant*, Leçon du 11 décembre 1973. (*The Seminar Book XXI. Les non-dupes errant*, Tuesday 11 December 1973, p. 76. Translation by Cormac Gallagher.)

14 Lacan, J., *Le Séminaire, Livre XXI. Les non-dupes errant*, leçon du 21 juin 1974. (*The Seminar Book XXI: Les non-dupes errant*, Tuesday 21 June 1974. p. 20.)

15 Lacan, J., *Le Séminaire, Livre XXI. Les non-dupes errant*, leçon du 18 décembre 1973. (*The Seminar Book XXI: Les non-dupes errant*, Tuesday 18 December 1973, p. 82.)

16 Lacan, J., « L'étourdit », in *Autres écrits*, p. 452.

17 Lacan, J., « *Le Séminaire, Livre XVII, L'envers de la psychanalyse* », Paris, Le Seuil, 1991, p. 76. (*The Seminar of Jacques Lacan, Book XVII, Psychoanalysis upside down/The reverse side of psychoanalysis: 1969–1970*, pp. 152 and 258. Translation by C. Gallagher.)

18 https://en.wiktionary.org/wiki/burr.

19 Lacan, J., « *Note Italienne* », in *Autres écrits*, p. 311. ("Italian Note", p. 8. Translation by Susan Schwartz.)

20 Lacan, J., *Le Séminaire, Livre X, l'Angoisse*, p. 38. (*The Seminar of Jacques Lacan, Book X, Anxiety, 1963–1963*, p. 23. Translation by C. Gallagher.)

21 Lacan, J., *Le Séminaire, Livre XX, Encore*, p. 132. (*The Seminar of Jacques Lacan, Book XX, Encore, 1972–1973*, p. 16. Translation by C. Gallagher.)

22 Lacan, J., « L'étourdit », in *Autres écrits*, p. 452. ("The Letter 41", p. 39. Translation by C. Gallagher.)

23 Lacan, J., « L'étourdit », in *Autres écrits*, p. 452. ("The Letter 41", July 1972, p. 105. Translation by C. Gallagher.)

24 Lacan, J., « ... ou pire », in *Autres écrits*, Paris le Seuil, 2001, p. 551. My translation.

25 Lacan, J., Séminaire XXIV "La direction de la cure et les principes de son pouvoir", *Écrits*. Paris, Le Seuil, 2001, p. 613. (*Direction of the Treatment and the Principles of Its Power*, New York and London, W.W Norton, p. 512. Translated by B. Fink in collaboration with H. Fink and R. Grigg.)

26 Lacan, J., « Préface à l'édition anglaise du *Séminaire XI* », in *Autres écrits*, p. 572. ("Preface to the English Edition of Seminar XI". Translation by Alan Sheridan.)
27 Lacan, J., *Le Séminaire, Livre XXIII, Le sinthome*, p. 164. ("Joyce the Symptom", *The Sinthome: The Seminar of Jacques Lacan Book XXIII*. Polity Press, Cambridge, 2018, p. 144. Translation by A.R. Price.)
28 Lacan, J., *Le Séminaire, Livre XXIII, Le sinthome*, p. 38. ("On What Makes a Hole in the Real", *The Sinthome: The Seminar of Jacques Lacan Book XXIII*. Polity Press, Cambridge, 2018, p. 28. Translation by A.R. Price.)

Index

For Product Safety Concerns and Information please contact our EU
representative GPSR@taylorandfrancis.com
Taylor & Francis Verlag GmbH, Kaufingerstraße 24, 80331 München, Germany